THE OLD ROCKERS' HANDBOOK

First published in November 2013

A catalogue record for this book is available from the British Library

ISBN 978 0 85733 474 9

Library of Congress control card no 2013944259

Published by Haynes Publishing,
Sparkford, Yeovil, Somerset BA22 7JJ, UK
Tel: 01963 442030 Fax: 01963 440001
Int. tel: +44 1963 442030 Int. fax: +44 1963 440001
E-mail: sales@haynes.co.uk
Website: www.haynes.co.uk

Haynes North America Inc.,
861 Lawrence Drive, Newbury Park,
California 91320, USA

Printed and bound in the USA by Odcombe Press LP,
1299 Bridgestone Parkway, La Vergne, TN 37086

While every effort is taken to ensure the accuracy of the information given in this book, no liability can be accepted by the author or publishers for any loss, damage or injury caused by errors in, or omissions from, the information given.

THE OLD ROCKERS' HANDBOOK

ALL THE MATURE MUSICIAN NEEDS

CHRIS MAILLARD

HAYNES PUBLISHING

CONTENTS

RICK WAKEMAN

FOREWORD

There are so many ingredients that appear in the makeup of a rock musician, and indeed there are many kinds of rock musician.

Apart from the multiple instrument choice available to the aspiring 'wannabe', there are also so many different kinds of player... the amateur, the semi-professional, the professional, the short-lived rocker and those who carry on until they die.

There are also a lot of misconceptions about how to be successful. This sometimes gets mixed up with 'enjoyment'. Almost anybody who can tap their feet in time can learn to play something to some sort of self-gratifying standard, so rule number one is to be honest with yourself as to what your true potential and ability is.

The main ingredient (and the one sadly lacking in much of current rock music) is that of natural talent. This seems to have been taken over by a mixture of 'ego', reality television shows and executives in the music business not knowing a hatchet from a crotchet.

Having said all this, it's a dream of so many to become a 'rocker', and why not. The great thing is that there are so many different levels that can be attained. Simply learning three chords can mean you can almost instantly be part of a blues band (providing they're playing the blues in the same key that you've learned your three chords). Of course, if you learn another couple of thousand you can form a prog rock band, and if you've no idea what chords you're actually playing, you can form a jazz/rock fusion band.

There's no greater buzz than being in a band. Just make sure you're of a similar standard to the other members. If you're better than them, you'll end up moving on to another band, and if you're not as good as the rest of them, then sooner or later you'll be asked to leave!

There is one golden rule that applies to all would-be rockers and that is to enjoy yourself. If you're having fun and enjoying what you do, then there's a reasonable chance that those listening will as well.

I have to once again reiterate 'honesty'. Know your limitations, potential and ability, and if at the end of the day you have to admit you're lacking in all three, then I'm led to understand that selling insurance can be quite lucrative.

Finally, if you believe you have all the attributes, but truthfully you haven't, then self-disillusionment will always mean there's a career for you in banking.

Rick Wakeman
November 2013

CHAPTER 1

WELCOME, MY FRIENDS...

Why write this book? And why now? Well, one of the first pieces of advice any writer gets thrown at them is 'write what you know'. Which isn't an awful lot of use if you want to write the next James Bond thriller and you work in a greengrocer's shop in Leicester. "Bond adjusted the Walther PPK in his shoulder holster and expertly weighed the cabbage..."

But in this case it does apply perfectly. I'm exactly the sort of person who I hope will enjoy this book. I was in umpteen bands in my teens and twenties, but then life happened. Steady relationship, jobs, kids, mortgages... just the usual stuff, and much of it rewarding, fulfilling and generally A Fine Thing. But it doesn't leave a lot of room for music, so that tended to get squeezed out until my only contact with it was occasionally glancing at the thick layer of dust on the guitar before rushing past it to do something more important.

The people I used to be in a band with became people I occasionally had a pint with, or people I didn't see much any more, or people about whom I thought 'I wonder what happened to...?' once in a while.

But then, as happens, life started to run slightly more smoothly. Children grew up and found far more interesting things to do with their time than spend it with some grumpy old fart; work started to get more manageable and flexible; odd moments of leisure time began to appear.

And that's when the urge to do something musical started to resurface. I blew the dust off the guitar, tried to remember which way up to hold it, even put new strings on it eventually. A few ex-musician mates reappeared with the same sort of urge – part musical nostalgia, part creative itch-scratching, part curiosity to see if they could still actually do it.

Then it seemed a good time to get out and do a bit of playing, so a band was scraped together after a few false starts, rehearsals organised, gigs booked and, blimey, suddenly I was playing in front of people again. Some of whom were even enjoying it.

I mentioned the band to a few people, as you do, and was frankly astonished by how many sensible, sober-suited grown-ups suddenly went all misty-eyed and admitted to the ownership of a slightly underused drum kit, an infrequently played guitar or a dusty keyboard. Reactions to my confession of late-onset musicianship ranged from jealousy to admiration to frank amazement, but almost every ex-musician shared the itch to resume playing in some shape or form.

So I found myself dispensing advice and encouragement to a large number of aspiring middle-aged musos; but whether it was about where to find fellow players, how to book gigs, or what technological advances had happened since 1981, their common complaint was that 'I don't know where to find out about this sort of stuff any more.'

I'd worked on several musicians' magazines back in the late Jurassic period and kept vaguely up to date with developments since, so with that, plus finding out quite a few practical things the hard way, I could often be of some help. But it was clear that there was a need for a decent source of information and inspiration for the more mature player.

There are plenty of books on musical heroes (and sometimes villains). There are also a good number of coffee-table volumes full of beautifully photographed, lovingly described vintage gear (or 'guitar porn' as it's more commonly known).

However, there was nothing that appealed more widely to the older strummer, banger or blower. There hasn't been a book that they, their partners or friends, could buy to let them know that it's perfectly OK to scratch your musical creative itch after a certain age, then give them the knowledge to do it without embarrassing themselves and everybody else.

So here's one. If it inspires a few people to get out and have some noisy fun, it'll have done its job.

Off you go then. 1–2–3–4...

SIDETRACK: OLDER PLAYERS

'Too old to rock 'n' roll, too young to die.' 'I hope I die before I get old.' 'Die young, stay pretty.' Those lyrics, surely, prove that popular music is a young person's game. If you're over 27, you're well past it.

But hang on – the people who sang those words are respectively 65, 68 and 67, and all of them are still gigging. Jethro Tull's Ian Anderson, The Who's Roger Daltrey and Blondie's Debbie Harry certainly haven't taken their own advice too seriously.

What's more, you might still catch B.B. King (87) Pete Seeger (93) or Leonard Cohen (78) on stage showing exactly why they're timelessly talented.

So if you're a current, lapsed or aspiring musician and you're thinking 'I'm a bit old for this lark', you're wrong.

Of course, you're not getting any younger. Nobody is. (If you have a secret trick that contradicts this, however, feel free to get in touch with the details. No, not you, L'Oréal).

The fact is that as a population, we're getting older. The baby boom is now a granny bulge. The drug-crazed hippies of the Summer of Love are now queueing up in Boots for cod liver oil.

But we're not willing to let go of the things we've enjoyed all the way through our lives. And why should we? The days when you hit some sort of middle-aged cliff-edge and suddenly tumbled over into a world of cardigans, lawnmowers and Horlicks are, thankfully, long gone.

One of the major things we've enjoyed is, of course, music. We're still listening to music, and the people who make that music are still producing it. In some cases they're gently replaying their earlier hits, in others they're releasing new music that's as surprising and challenging as ever (greetings Mr Bowie, 66) and others seem to be hitting yet another creative peak. Did anyone else think that the last few Robert Plant albums were extremely good? He's 64, by the way. Neil Young (67) isn't slowing down too much either, judging by the ferocious guitar freakouts on his most recent album.

So what's the secret to their musical longevity? There doesn't seem to be a simple single answer – except that they've all kept their enthusiasm, curiosity and musical flexibility.

Would you have put the frontman of heavy rock monarchs Led Zeppelin down as an admirer of bluegrass? Could you have guessed that '60s pop icon Marianne Faithfull (66) would build a very fine career in later life including a collaboration with Metallica? Or that genial slide guitar legend Ry Cooder (66) would record one of the most acerbic and hard-hitting political protest albums of the past decade?

There are many other great examples of restless, genre-hopping musicians who haven't let their maturity get in the way of staying fresh and having new ideas.

That seems to be what it's all about – staying flexible. Maybe that cod liver oil is a good idea. As a musician, or a would-be musician yourself, the lesson's an easy one. Stay curious; don't get locked into old habits and keep your eyes open for exciting fresh things, whether they're the latest bands or whole new musical areas. Explore blues, country, soul and anything else that takes your fancy; it'll all feed back into your playing and give you a unique, interesting perspective on music.

And most of all, stay fresh. Apparently Tupperware's handy...

CHAPTER 2

WEAPON OF CHOICE

What instrument do you want to play? Yes, it sounds like a silly question if you've been a guitarist, drummer or harpsichordist since you were six years old, but if you're just starting to think about getting involved in music, or rekindling a long-dormant interest, it's definitely worth considering.

And even if you think you know what you play, is it the only option? Could you widen your musical horizons, or your potential choice of bands or musical collaborators, by learning something else as well? Or switch to a different specialism? All worth a good think, so here's a rough guide to the pros and cons of each of the major instruments you're likely to run across. No, triangle players, I'm afraid you don't get a separate section. Though if enough of you write in maybe I could add one specifically on things that go 'ting!' and look idiotic.

You might be tempted to slide past this bit if you're already dedicated to one particular instrument, but hang on – what if you want to do a bit of home recording? Or what about adding a few different colours to your palette? Guitarists are fairly lucky, in that they can apply quite a bit of their existing knowledge to other plucked string instruments from the banjo to the lap steel, the ukelele to the mandolin. But so can bass players. Keyboard players will find that they have a good overall knowledge of theory, thanks to the tidy layout of a keyboard, which can be transferred to many other instruments. Every drummer should have a working knowledge of bass, and vice versa, so when you need to lock together as a rhythm section you know what you're playing off. And so on. Don't get stuck in a musical rut; explore a bit. And if you find yourself getting bored with practising your existing instrument, an excursion into unfamiliar parts can stop you suffering from terminal tedium and freshen up your playing. It's like a little holiday for the fingers.

If you're a novice or hugely rusty, it's also worth thinking about how much time you've got to learn, relearn or add to your mastery of your chosen instrument. Some are relatively quick to pick up, others will take a long course of lessons and some seriously dedicated practice. Want to get really, really good on the oboe, the cor anglais or the harp? You might want to start about 25 years ago. You could probably master the basics of the one-string bottleneck guitar, however, before you reach the end of this sentence. There, got it.

So here's your guide to the major noisemakers. Take your pick. If you're a guitarist, of course, you will anyway.

GUITAR

This is the big one, isn't it? Guitar – the instrument all the real megastars play. After all, who ever heard of a videogame called Piano Hero? It's a posing tool, a talent magnet, an ego booster with six strings and a worryingly phallic shape.

But hang on a minute. Now you're a little too old to pose in front of the mirror with a tennis racket (at least without feeling mildly embarrassed), are you entirely sure that the guitar's not a little too obvious, a bit of a well-trodden path?

You fancy being a guitarist. But... you're not the first person to have had this idea. You're not the millionth. You're probably not even the ten millionth. Guitars are everywhere, like six-stringed cockroaches, inescapable and unkillable. Go to any blues jam or folk open mic night and you'll find two bass players, three drummers, a singer and about 140 guitarists. And it's almost impossible to strum a few chords on a guitar without stumbling across a horrible cliché. If you want originality, you're forced to play it with a baseball bat or tune it to infeasibly complicated Tibetan intervals. Because everything else has been done. Everything.

Still not put off? That's fine. It was worth a go. Playing the guitar may not be the most original thing you can do, but it can be a gigantic amount of fun.

The guitar has huge advantages, which is probably why it became so ridiculously popular in the first place. It's fairly portable, it's widely accepted as being vaguely cool and it's relatively easy to make a noise that is roughly similar to your musical heroes.

The acoustic guitar is about the right volume for accompanying a singer's voice or playing quietly at home without causing a riot, and its electric cousin offers a wide range of options, from gritty blues rhythm to spacy effects-laden weirdness, and from twangy rockabilly licks to all-out rawwwkkkkk lunacy.

Guitars come in a dizzying range of sizes, colours, shapes, configurations and options. Want one in luminous pink, shaped like a butterfly's backside and equipped with three necks? It's almost certainly out there somewhere (hint: check your local prog-rock superstar's attic). They come covered in dust, dirt and grime, redolent of delta mojo and beery barroom sweat, or immaculate and futuristic, like the music-mad love child of Concorde and a Dyson vacuum.

Learning the guitar is a well-worn path, with umpteen teachers' details on every music shop noticeboard and so many internet video tutorials that if you watched them all you'd never have time to actually play the thing. With three chords you're equipped to tackle most blues songs, about half of the folk repertoire and 95% of the classic punk anthems.

And then you can start improving, whether it's painstaking knuckle-twisting fingerpicking runs you want to tackle or note-by-note unpicking and reassembly of classic electric solos.

Or you can learn the bare minimum necessary to crash through a song or two, then get out and entertain an audience, from your long-suffering family through the punters of open mic nights and club support sets and finally, maybe, even some people who have actually turned up and paid their own money to listen to you play.

You do need perseverance and a little talent, a reasonable ear and some dexterity, but the guitar can make even the minimally gifted look more or less competent and sound fairly acceptable. What's not to like?

BASS

The bass is the secret weapon of any band. It's often hardly noticeable unless you listen closely, and many of its players are equally backward at coming forward. It's a vital half of the rhythm section, but doesn't usually match the drummer's sweaty energetic antics, and is often roundly ignored by fans and other band members alike.

So why on earth would anybody choose to play the bass? Well, for some of those reasons. If you're the sort of musician who doesn't mind being a little under the radar, it's perfect. There's a sort of absorbing, trance-like satisfaction to laying down a good bassline, locking in seamlessly with the drum pattern and propelling a song forwards. It's an introvert's dream; you can be part of the onstage action without having to be the one in the embarrassing trousers at the front (not always, though – check out Thin Lizzy's Phil Lynott, Iron Maiden's Steve Harris and Rush's Geddy Lee for three superb exponents of bass-plus-silly-legwear action).

And though being a great bass player is a life's work, being a more or less competent one is not too tricky. If you already play a little guitar, you're most of the way there. The rather cruel gag 'a bass player is just a guitarist who can't count up to six' is founded on a true fact; it's the bottom four strings of a guitar, without the faff of playing chords. If you've got a solid sense of rhythm and a decent instinct for when not to play, bass is a very good, simple bet.

Of course, you can go further than that; there's fretless bass, for those who feel that being entirely in tune is too much of a restriction to their creative freedom; five- or slx-strng bass for those who want to induce spontaneous and violent diarrhoea in their audience; acoustic bass for wholegrain folkies; that weird but atmospheric hybrid, baritone guitar; keyboard bass for those with supernatural left/right hand co-ordination and a liking for The Doors; pedal bass for skilled tap-dancers; and of course double bass, for bequiffed rockabillies, retro jazzers and classical cats. Beware, though – that last one brings with it all sorts of practical considerations, from complex and expensive pickup/microphone systems to enable you to be heard above a modern band, finger callouses and temperamental bits of woodwork, to the simple fact that you're trying to cart around something the size and weight of a garden shed. Got a car? Got a really, really big car? You'll need one. That or a moped engine, a skateboard and some rubber bands.

But however inconvenient bass playing can be, or however straightforward it seems at first, it can be terribly addictive. There's something about the combination of apparent simplicity and actual indispensability that gets under the skin. You can be standing modestly in the shadows off to one side of the stage, but in reality you're the centre of any band, linking the rhythm to the melody, supplying the essential propulsive energy and allowing space to happen when needed, driving the song forward and setting the tempo and feel.

Still think it's just a series of dull woofy noises? Your loss. Have a go and see what you're missing.

DRUMS
What can you say about drums? I SAID WHAT CAN... Oh, never mind.

Firstly, they're really flipping loud. For many years there was no alternative to this immense volume and bassists went deaf, singers strained to hear themselves, and guitar players hid behind walls of competing amps. Now there are fairly decent, reasonably convincing electronic kits which have a volume knob that actually goes both ways. But at its most basic, you're dealing with the sound of somebody walloping an object with a stick. That's never going to be a terribly quiet thing.

Secondly, they're very physical. No matter how lively strummers, pickers and blowers may get, nothing compares with the sheer physical effort of thrashing two sticks and two pedals, or whatever your kit features, for pretty much the entire duration of a show. It's hard on the wrists, the back, the shoulders and the knees; there are even several particularly nasty complaints you can get from spending too long perched on sweaty drum stools. Best left to the imagination, that; just don't think too hard about it before eating.

And thirdly, they're the foundation of almost every type of music. There's a broad range of styles from Neanderthal rock skin-bashers to twiddly, earnest jazz intellectuals, super-funky offbeat specialists to lightning-wristed latin percussionists, and yet reduced to its basics it's all about the backbeat, the driving force of the sound and the rhythmic cue for dancing, moshing, pogoing or whatever physical reaction your music demands (for the more complex styles of jazz, I suggest an almost imperceptible nod of approval on every other offbeat, if you can find it. But don't dislodge your Ray-Bans).

Drummers are also, of course, the butt of a classic

series of hoary old jokes, which we will pass over silently. Oh no we won't. Here are the three oldest and crustiest, probably:

Q: What do you call somebody who hangs around with musicians?
A: A drummer.

Q: How can you tell when the stage is level?
A: The drummer dribbles from both sides of his mouth.

Q: How can you tell when there's a drummer at the door?
A: The knocking gets faster towards the end.

There are hundreds more, from knock-knock jokes to shaggy dog stories. If you're a drummer, or thinking of becoming one, just get used to it. Or find your own stock of bass player jokes, singer jokes, guitarist jokes etc and retaliate.

So you get sweaty and you get insulted. Why ever would you become a drummer? Simple. It's huge fun. There's some part of the brain that really likes hitting things, enjoys rhythm and gets off on the co-ordination involved in keeping a complex groove going. And the best drummers combine brute force, talent and intelligence in a way that no other musician can. Watching a great drummer push and pull the beat, control the dynamics and hit the perfect groove is awe-inspiring; doing it yourself, even though you may not be quite in the legendary category yet, is exciting and exhilarating.

Yes, you have to cart a large set of heavy boxes around and bolt them together at every gig or rehearsal. Yes, you have to put in a gym session's worth of exertion while everyone else is barely twitching. Yes, you occasionally get treated like a member of some sort of subhuman musical underclass.

But despite all that, being a drummer is a unique, addictive and extremely satisfying thing. You can't beat it. Oh, you just did.

KEYS

If you already play any instrument, no matter what, there's one more you should learn that will improve your musical skill and knowledge – the keyboard.

The great thing about any keyboard instrument is that all the notes are laid out in front of you. With a guitar, you're continually calculating which strings and frets create which note or chord; with wind instruments it's all about combining valves, levers or stops. On a keyboard, though, it's simple. Hit a key, there it is. Suddenly, musical theory starts to make sense. Oh, that's how a seventh works. A major third? There it is. Easy.

Being able to pick out a few notes on a keyboard won't make you into the new Beethoven immediately, of course, but having one as a second instrument will help make whatever else you do seem less mysterious and theoretical.

Playing a keyboard as your main instrument, though, is a choice that immediately seems to put you into the intellectual camp, whether it's the classically cool piano, the boffin-approved synthesiser or even the sleazy rasp of the organ.

One reason is that ease of access to all the notes; it makes complex chords and clever inversions effortless for the theoretically minded. Many keyboard players come from a background of classical music, which immediately brings with it a rather un-rock 'n' roll knowledge of theory.

The other is that dynamics on a keyboard instrument are a little limited. While a good acoustic piano is of course touch-sensitive, its dynamic range is nowhere near that of most other instruments, which can easily go from a barely audible whisper to a deafening scream. With most electric pianos, organs and synths there's even less choice: your volume is determined entirely by a pedal or a knob rather than how hard or soft your playing is. This can make keyboard instruments, played insensitively, seem rather clinical and soulless. Dynamics take more deliberate thought than with many instruments, though they're by no means impossible.

But keyboards make up for that mild limitation with their vast, almost endless, range of sounds. Given a sampler, a good synth or a software emulator there's not much you can't reproduce. Not that you should, of course. Playing your showcase solo in the voice of Donald Duck is funny. Once. The second time round, physical violence is a likely outcome. The third time? Well, no court in the land would hand down a murder conviction given the evidence.

Keyboard instruments come in all shapes and sizes, are easy to practise noiselessly with headphones on (unless you insist on only playing a grand piano, of course, you poser) and if your left/right hand independence is well developed you don't even need a band to produce a full-sounding bass and melody combo all by yourself. Why not play a keyboard? It's a black and white decision. Oh.

WIND

Stop sniggering at the back, there. There's nothing funny about farting and burping. Well, maybe there is. But all wind players have, I'm sure, heard every variation on those gags about four million times.

That's one of the downsides of playing a wind instrument. The positives, however, are many. For a start, some of the coolest musicians ever were wind players. Miles Davis. John Coltrane. The doomed star Chet Baker, who had more cool in his left eyebrow than most entire bands can muster. Even art-rock megastar David Bowie plays a mean sax.

There's a tremendous range, too, from reeds (saxophone, oboe, bassoon, clarinet – and not forgetting the harmonica) to brass (trumpet, trombone, euphonium, flugelhorn, tuba, bugle, cor anglais and so on) and on into flutes, recorders, ocarinas and, yes, the mighty kazoo and swanee whistle, comedy instruments par excellence.

Somewhere in this lot is something you'll have a liking for, whether it's Junior Parker-style sassy R&B or Count Basie's big band brass. And the harmonica (aka blues harp) is out on its own in terms of portability, ease of playing and instant delta cred.

So where to start? With a teacher, is the answer. Most of these instruments are relatively complex and come complete with lots of fiddly levers, holes, valves and other gadgets of the sort that you might expect to find on a model steam engine. So you need someone to show you the basics and go through which bit does what.

Embouchure, or 'lip' is vital to playing most of these instruments properly too – getting your tongue, teeth and chops to do the right things takes quite some practice, and somebody who knows what they're doing can short-cut that process pretty well.

Once you've picked up the basics, though, you do run into another small snag – most wind instruments are loud, and therefore practising at four in the morning in a thin-walled flat will not get you many votes for Neighbour of the Year. They're actually designed to be loud – the saxophone was specifically built to honk its way to the front of a military marching band's racket – but that's not going to cheer up your frazzled cohabitants much. There are mutes and 'silent' practice instruments, but it's not quite the same thing. You'll have to find somewhere to practise – schools are often a good bet – or maybe lock yourself in a wardrobe. No, really. You could always stuff an item of clothing in the bell of your instrument (hence the saying 'put a sock in it'), which helps a bit, but basically you're stuck with an instrument with immense acoustic volume. This, however, will save you a fortune in amplification when you do play with any but the most excessively noisy bands.

The likelihood, though, is that if you're veering towards a wind instrument your record collection is unlikely to include vast amounts of death metal or hardcore thrash. Jazz is, of course, the happy hunting ground of most wind players and there's a pretty good range even if you just stick to that genre, from gentle trad meandering to fierce hard bop and the twiddly intricacies of jazz-fusion. But reggae, soul, blues, classic pop and folk all offer a place for wind instruments. And who's to say you couldn't start the first bassoon-led thrash-metal outfit? I'd pay money to see that (but not all that much).

There's one oddity in the wind department, however, and that's the harmonica. Though a few brave players have tried to slide into jazz (you really should check out Larry Adler's astonishing skills), it's so associated with blues that it works as an immediate signal – any time someone wants to conjure up deep southern poverty or big city lowlife, out comes the harmonica and everybody immediately gets the idea. It can add a bit of blues flavour to hard rock too – many supergroups from the Rolling Stones to Led Zeppelin, Free to Deep Purple, weren't averse to a bit of mouth harp here and there.

It's also unique among wind instruments in that there's a thriving culture of harmonica players with loud electric bands who use amplification, distortion and sometimes effects as an essential part of their tone. The idea of fuzzed flute may be more than a little peculiar, but adding some valve-driven grit to a blues harp's sound seems to work well, and of course adds much-needed volume when you're competing against a lead-fisted drummer and a power-crazed guitarist or two.

But whether you go for the traditional end of wind or amp up and rock out, you'll always be in demand; once you get good, paid gigs are quite possible and swapping between bands is perfectly accepted. If you want to play every night of the week, you could probably, er, swing it. So, do you get wind now (snigger)?

STRINGS

By which we mean anything that has strings on it, or in it, but isn't a guitar or bass. Not much choice left there, surely? Wrong.

It encompasses the classical instruments like violin, cello, viola, or harp (hello, Florence). It also brings in the folky favourites such as bouzoukis and mandocellos, mandolins and fiddles, banjos and ukeleles. And over on the extreme wing of the world music faction, there's a whole universe of ouds and sazes, sitars and balalaikas, charangos and tiples. Having a medieval moment? There are lutes and dulcimers, psalteries and hurdy-gurdies, viols and citterns. And there's more. From the deepest of bluegrass and its Appalachian dulcimers, auto-harps and zithers, to the futuristic, tapped, multi-octave Chapman Stick, and from the one-string blues minimalism of the diddley bow to the terrifying complexity of country's pedal steel with its knee levers and multiple necks, there are so many things with strings that it's hard to know where to start, or which end to pluck. Or bow. Or fret.

'Strings', as in 'cue the strings' or 'are the string section in the pub again?' is often loosely used to refer to a classical set of bowed instruments: violin, viola, cello, sometimes a bowed double bass too. They're often pigeonholed as a clichéd accompaniment to weepy ballads and soggy love songs, but are capable of so much more; check out Elvis Costello's album with the Brodsky Quartet or the unfairly obscure American singer Alejandro Escovedo, who often plays his border rock 'n' roll with a string quartet live. Deceased folk hero Nick Drake's 'Cello Song' is not only another great showcase, but even named after its featured instrument. So if your background is from the world of classical strings, don't immediately throw the viola in a cupboard and reach for a Stratocaster; consider whether you could add a distinctive flavour to more modern music.

Or, of course, you could always change the name of your instrument from 'violin' to 'fiddle' and dive into the world of folk, celtic music or bluegrass. There's plenty of scope there to hop from Stravinsky's twiddly bits to wild Irish reels and jigs, or for that matter from Aaron Copeland's orchestral Americana to the prairie sounds of country or bluegrass.

Usefully, many stringed instruments, from folk favourites to obscure world music oddities, can be loosely arranged into families which share tunings or playing styles. If you master one of a family, it's easier to get the hang of more. And that itself can influence your playing on a more standard instrument. Folk is full of irritatingly talented multi-instrumentalists who can hop seemingly effortlessly between guitar and banjo, mandolin and open-tuned resonator. Having to deal with different tunings, scale lengths and right-hand techniques ought to be deeply confusing, but it can actually sharpen up your understanding of the basics, which helps your playing right across the board. Or the fretboard.

If you're a guitar player but you feel you're not getting anywhere, why not try another in the same family of instruments? Banjo will do wonders for your right-hand speed and precision, mandolin will supercharge your plectrum style, and even the tiny ukelele will force you to strip your playing down to basics and rethink chord patterns. Plus, it's ultra-portable so will double your opportunities to practise.

If you're an electric blues or country player, broaden your horizons (and possibly your buttocks) by sitting down. No, really – lap steel or pedal steel, while played seated, are an exercise in rethinking the idea of guitar, but still within those familiar scales and sounds. Listen closely to Ry Cooder or David Lindley and prepare to have your mind thoroughly expanded without leaving your seat. Or steer away from the multi-stringed mind-boggler that is pedal steel, drive a nail into a plank and make your own diddley bow – a one-stringed wonder, played with a slide, that is the essence of primitive blues boiled down to its very basics. Couldn't be simpler, but surprisingly versatile and absorbing; perfect for back porches, beach bonfires and spooky murder ballads at midnight.

And there's much more. Delve into world music's strings department and you're in for an amazing international head trip. If you're anywhere near a branch of folk and world music specialists Hobgoblin Music, drop in and spend an hour or so checking out their menagerie of odd instruments. Come on, don't you want a go on a cümbüş or a vihuela? Or at least a shot at learning how to pronounce them?

And remember, if it's got strings and you already

play something else with strings it's not going to be that tricky to pick up (let's try to ignore the hideously complicated hurdy-gurdy here, which is a sort of hybrid of bagpipes, an inside-out cello and a wind-up gramophone, with a bit of sewing machine and some sitar thrown in for good luck).

So give it a go. Get plucking, or bowing. Extend your range, expand your mind, stretch your technique and get further into the wonderful world of strings. What can possibly go wrong? Oh bugger, I've just snapped the top C string on my shamisen. That, obviously.

VOCALS

There are two opposing schools of thought on singing. One goes 'anyone can do it' and the other goes 'good singers are very rare'.

Annoyingly, both are valid. At least partly. It's certainly true that almost everybody can make a sort of noise that resembles singing. It may not be entirely in tune, it may be very loose in terms of timing and it may have all the timbre and texture of somebody torturing a goose, but it's still, technically, singing.

On the other hand, a really good singer can take the same vocal line and render it accurately, attractively and effortlessly.

Which are you? Well, if you haven't done it before, or you haven't done it for years, or you don't feel confident doing it, then your singing is highly likely to fall into the goose-strangling category. That effortlessness doesn't just happen, you know – there's a lot of effort behind it.

One of the major obstacles most singers face is

confldence. It takes quite a bit of bottle to stand up in front of people you don't know, armed with nothing other than a pair of lungs and a dollop of hope, and belt out a song or several. A microphone stand is way too small to hide behind (unless you're extremely thin) and if you're the lead singer you're usually stuck at the front, illuminated by a spotlight and trying hard not to lose control of your bowels.

This, it is often claimed, gets better with practice. Some singers would beg to differ; for many people, the 250th gig is just as nerve-wracking as the first. However, what does improve is your level of confidence in your material and your voice's technical ability. But it's surprising how many well-practised singers still get the wobbles before going on stage. There is, of course, a possibly unexpected answer to this.

Singing is still seen as something entirely artless; you just open your mouth and, if you've got the gift, a pleasing sound comes out. This is, frankly, cobblers. You need to practise singing frequently and in a disciplined way, just as you do any musical instrument.

And if you're at all serious about it, you will almost certainly find lessons to be very helpful to both your confidence and your technical ability. The best singing teachers find a way to make your voice work more reliably and more accurately, but even more beneficial is that they can often find ways to give a singer the vital sense of security in their ability, a safety net which makes for a confident, competent performance.

If you've ever fancied singing (and who hasn't entertained the occasional fantasy about being the centre of attention, or at least to be able to belt out some decent backing vocals?) it's well worth having an exploratory lesson or two to find out if you're made of the right stuff.

A singing teacher may claim that they can teach anybody to sing. This might well be true. Can they teach anybody to sing in a way you want to listen to? More difficult. You may be a born goose-strangler.

But if you don't try it, you'll never know. You might just be the next Robert Plant, Billie Holiday or Tim Buckley. Or you might just find out that your singing voice sounds like Bob Dylan gargling with marbles. Still, at least you'll know...

THE REST

Or 'None of the Above', if you prefer. But hang on, we've covered guitar, bass, drums, keyboards, wind instruments, strings and even vocals. What's left?

Well, the xylophone (and its cousins the glockenspiel and marimba) hasn't really had much of a look-in. Is it because it's too close to the end of the alphabet? No, I think we mentioned the zither once, and that's even further down.

The accordion and concertina somehow escaped too. Even if polka, zydeco and sea shanties are all fine genres, none have really made the mainstream of late. And the necessity of growing an enormous beard and having a wooden leg to add authenticity to your songs of life on the ocean wave puts some people off. Particularly women.

We haven't really covered pure percussion either; although it starts off in the general direction of drums, it expands into a whole new set of areas including world music and experimental jazz, with polyrhythmic patterns and textural soundscapes equally possible. But that's sort of hair-splitting (except with more cowbell).

And we haven't delved into the area of computers and sampling much yet. Yes, the usual method of accessing the software is via a keyboard (of either type), but this is much less about playing an instrument and more about producing and processing noises, sequencing and slicing to create a piece of music which would quite likely be physically impossible to replicate using conventional instruments and which involves entirely synthetic ingredients. Ever heard anybody busking dubstep? No, thought not.

However, if this rings your sampled and heavily processed bell there's a thriving subculture of laptop musicians that diverges wildly from the meat-and-potatoes guitar band gig circuit and uses sites like Soundcloud, Freesound and Soundation to foster online collaboration and entirely eliminate the need to have a bunch of sweaty musicians in a small room at the same time. This may well be a good thing, unless you're a deodorant manufacturer.

But what if you're deeply enthusiastic about music, but simply not bothered about playing an instrument or singing due to cack-handedness, tone-deafness or a bad attack of can't-be-arsed and too-late-to-learn? None of the above means that you can't get involved. The rude and cynical would say 'just become a drummer' (see drummer jokes earlier on in this chapter for more top-class rudeness) but we won't stoop so low.

Instead, how about taking on one of the many backroom roles in music – management, sound engineering, booking, DJing, maybe acting as a stage technician or roadie? All of these are vital, all are fascinating – though you may beg to differ if you've somehow ended up heaving a stack of speaker cabinets out of a venue at 2am – and all can be tackled without the tedious necessity of practising an instrument obsessively for years.

Bands, you see, need people who aren't musicians to make stuff happen. There are famous examples: producer George Martin was often referred to as 'the fifth Beatle'; many West Coast artists like Joni Mitchell and Neil Young credit their success to legendary manager David Geffen; and REM's road manager and friend Jefferson Holt even became immortalised in song when his rather random map-reading skills prompted the song 'Little America' with its rueful final line "Jefferson, I think we're lost."

If you know any musicians, just mention that you might be able to help out then stand well back while they jump at the chance. Every band or artist needs a team of people to take care of business, but few actually do have. Whether it's driving the van or mixing the sound, it'll be extremely welcome.

Or if you happen to know of a local pub or venue that's underused or disorganised, why not think about putting on a night or two there? If you're reasonably sorted, there's no reason why you can't see some excellent bands, get to make some new friends, drink free beer, and even make a small amount of money in the process. Notice the word 'small' there. The live circuit isn't exactly a gold mine, but if you're fairly careful and smart you can come out of it with enough to pay your expenses and subsidise the occasional post-gig curry.

In short, whether you're a musician or not there's no reason to stay in every night staring at some rubbish reality TV show or other. Get out, get active, get involved. Go on then, get on with it.

CHAPTER 3

START ME UP

You've got an instrument. Or a voice. You've got some idea of what your tastes are, and a hankering to do some vague musical stuff. But what?

That's the question. There's a yawning gap between that tickly sensation somewhere at the base of the brain that nags away, making you want to scratch some sort of musical itch, and actually stepping out on a stage in front of people to perform.

That is, of course, if your particular itch includes performing. It may not; you may just want to produce a pleasingly professional and personally satisfying recording. You may feel that the whole point of the process is to get together with a gang of friends, where playing music is just an excuse to have a few beers and a laugh, or you may have a burning desire to put your songwriting skills, musical talent and artistic vision across to as large a number of people as possible.

Or you might just want to sit in the spare bedroom and worry away at your technique, painstakingly improving your playing note by note until you reach some sort of personal goal – even if it's just to keep on improving.

Whatever your particular ambition, there's a way to achieve it (if you're going for Best Musician in the World Ever this may take a little longer, of course). You just have to decide what you actually want to do, and find a sensible and manageable route to get there.

So here are your various options, complete with pros and cons, explored and thoroughly assessed. Somewhere in this giant all-you-can-eat buffet of possibilities is the perfect one, or two, or three, for you. Because while there's more than one way to skin a cat (sorry, cat lovers) there are even more ways to scratch that musical itch, and you may fancy flitting between several of them to find that satisfying combination that's just right for you.

Here goes then. Whatever you want, as the great Status Quo put it – and that's a band that obviously had a clear ambition in mind. Even if it never included learning that difficult fourth chord.

JOIN A BAND

This is the obvious thing to do. But it's also a fine thing to do. It may be the only logical thing to do, if you're a particular kind of musician; opportunities for unaccompanied bass playing or solo drumming are few and far between.

It's a choice fraught with compromises and potential conflicts, but it can also be a uniquely enjoyable experience, fusing team spirit and musical talent to produce something magical, surprising and far greater than the sum of its parts.

However, even within the seemingly simple idea of joining a band there are all sorts of alternatives and variations, so let's tackle a few of them.

First, the most obvious – join an existing band. This sounds easy. It may not prove quite so straightforward, though. One of the things about bands is that often they're only partially about the music. This varies from band to band; some are certainly sternly professional outfits who rarely communicate other than to discuss rehearsal times, arrangements and chord voicings, and who wouldn't dream of getting their social life mixed up with their musical work.

Others, though, are a combination of club, drinking team, best mates and musical collaborators. They meet in the pub, they know all about each other's lives, partners, families, jobs and football teams and the band functions as just another reason to socialise with some enjoyable company.

So which would you prefer? If you're strongly attracted to one end of the spectrum or the other and end up joining a band with the opposite orientation, it can all get a bit miserable. The 'it's all about the music' contingent will think you're a bit of a lightweight if you come across as too sociable; the 'mates with guitars' lot will get the impression you're a snooty git if you spurn their invitations for a pint in favour of an extra hour studying your chord sheets. Choose carefully. This is not always easy to divine from an advert or even an audition, so probe your potential bandmates' motivations and attitudes when you get a chance to sit down for a proper conversation with them.

And when you do that, also try to get an idea of the personal dynamics within the band. The cliché runs as follows: Egotistical, image-obsessed singer; touchy, ambitious guitarist; pointy-headed, aloof keyboard player; long-suffering, silent bass player; irrepressible, utterly bonkers drummer.

If that's your band, sorry. It's surprising how often that particular cliché turns out to be true, or nearly so. But it's also tempting to try and slot band members into those specific roles, even if they don't fit anywhere near as neatly as that. So don't take fellow musicians at face value, and try to switch on your personality antenna before stereotyping them.

Of course, you also need to try and spot any potential troublemakers before it's too late. The term 'musicians' can also include psychopaths, sociopaths, substance abusers, criminals, serial pisstakers, nasty drunks, the cripplingly cynical, the painfully shy, the wilfully unreliable, the permanently bankrupt, the violent, the amoral and the borderline insane. And that was just my last band.

But assuming you manage to avoid all those booby traps and find yourself in a band who are roughly on your wavelength, share some musical influences and can play at more or less your level of competence, there's one more hurdle, which is the practical side of running a band. Sometimes this falls on the shoulders of one person, usually the bandleader or driving force behind the band, but often jobs like booking gigs, organising rehearsals, printing posters and so on are shared out between anybody who's got a bit of spare time. Which may mean you, so be prepared to step up and pull your weight. One really good way of annoying other members of your band, sometimes to the point of sacking you, leaving or just disbanding entirely, is to be useless luggage, evading any responsibility and shirking your chores. Don't do it. But if you do have to swerve some bit of band-related work, make sure you're clear about why, and pass it on swiftly with a promise to pick up the slack next time. The last thing you need is to turn up just before a gig and find somebody going "But I thought *you* were going to bring the bass amp...".

Or worse, still, not to turn up to a gig at all because somebody forgot to mention it. Or you forgot to put it in your diary. Be organised and thoughtful, though, and it'll all be OK.

There is an alternative to joining a band, of course, even if you still want to play along with other musicians – and that's forming your own. This is the favoured route for massive egotists, would-be fascist dictators, people with unique and unpopular musical tastes and terrible control freaks, but even if you don't fit into any (or all) of those categories, it's well worth considering.

For a start, you're not dealing with any of the luggage from previous band members. The line "...but our old guitarist/drummer/singer/bassist didn't do it like that" gets very, very tedious very, very quickly. And the fact that your predecessor in the band may have had major issues shouldn't really be your problem, but somehow is. Why were they sacked exactly? Was it that thing with the aubergine and the sack of kittens? Why are you looking at me like that?

Starting your own band also means that you can begin with a clean sheet of paper musically. If you've got a well-defined musical direction in mind, you can find other players who share that and can contribute to it. Alternatively, you can find players who you get on well with personally, then allow the sound to grow organically as a product of everybody's joint styles and influences.

Also, you can mess about with the standard formula if you want. Not happy with the traditional guitar–bass–drums line-up? Find an alternative. There was one tremendous band during the '90s called Morphine who comprised a drummer, a baritone sax player and a singer who played a home-built two-string bass guitar. With a slide. As Barry Norman used to say, "And why not?"

Starting your own band is more hard work than just stepping into someone else's footsteps, but can be more rewarding too. The sense of achievement from playing your first gig with a started-from-scratch outfit is definitely a notch or two above just continuing with an existing band's line-up.

But whichever way you go, provided you've chosen wisely, the combination of personal camaraderie and musical collaboration should produce a result that is both enjoyable and listenable. Unless you've gone for a three banjo, piccolo flute and glockenspiel line-up of course. Which you're completely entitled to do. Your band, your rules. Now if you'll excuse me, something important's come up just out of earshot...

GO SOLO

This is, frankly, terrifying. At least for many people it is. If you're nervous enough on stage while supported by a gang of bandmates, imagine how bum-squeakingly frightened you'd be on your own, stuck in the spotlight, armed with only an instrument and a voice. Nowhere to run to, baby, nowhere to hide. That was Martha & the Vandellas, and at least there were three of them.

But stage fright is just one of the hurdles you have to

climb over as a solo artist; you also usually have to deal with being the only person responsible for gigs, gear, transport, accommodation, marketing, promotion, song choice or songwriting, finances and trying to remember where you put the spare strings.

Sounds dire? Actually, no. There is a singular satisfaction in doing your own thing and doing it well. You put in all the effort, but you reap all the rewards.

Audiences are notably kinder to a solo artist than a band; while the faceless roar of a group's sound can be impersonal and uninvolving, people recognise and appreciate the bravery and talent of a single person laying bare their feelings, making an entirely personal statement and testing their skill without the safety net of other musicians.

And you're not actually as alone as all that; while your turn in the spotlight may be a solo affair, you'll more than likely be part of a community of other singletons, whether at a singers' night or a folk club, who are generous with their support and encouragement. They know what an effort it is to get up and perform on your own for the first time, and warmly welcome new recruits to the singular society.

The classic musical solo act is, of course, a singer/guitarist. It might be a bit of a cliché, but that's because it works so well. A guitar is easily portable, can supply both rhythm and counter-melody to a voice, and makes a vast range of noises from bog-standard strumming to delicate fingerpicking, plaintive bottleneck to virtuoso chord vamping. It's widely accepted, from folk to country, blues and jazz, then into the wider world with flamenco, reggae, afrobeat, bluegrass and beyond. Also, it's not all that tricky to learn well enough to thrash out a rough approximation of a song or two.

The piano is, however, an alternative. Apart from the 'portable' bit, although a decent electric keyboard can be an acceptable substitute in a pianoless venue. It's still got a slightly more upmarket air; somehow, it lends more sophistication to a song than a guitar.

This may not be ideal if you're after a grubby, alternative edge. There's a bit of a gulf between Liberace and The Clash. It can also tip a sensitive singer-songwriter over the edge from emotional and heartfelt into twee and affected, and even a bluesy honky-tonk style can jar, as anyone will know who's witnessed Jools Holland ruining perfectly decent artists' performances by splashing loud tinkly-winkly piano runs all over the song. But a good piano performance is a fine thing, whether simple chords or complicated multi-octave runs.

There are other instruments that accompany the voice well, but are less widely used. The general rule of thumb is usually that they need to be polyphonic – in other words, able to play chords rather than single notes – have a wide enough range to supplement the human voice's middly wavelengths both above and below with bass and treble, and be playable while singing, without getting in the way too much.

Quite a few of the family of stringed instruments fall more or less within this rule: banjo, ukelele and dulcimer are all usable, and alt-country legend Steve Earle is currently rocking a bouzouki with great aplomb. Organs, harmoniums and other keyboard instruments generally work too. The accordion and concertina, though usually limited to certain styles of music, also fall well within the possibles category.

Like all rules, though, this one is made to be broken and plenty of people have. If you're prepared to alternate singing and blowing, the harmonica's a favourite. Doing both while also playing the guitar necessitates some scaffolding of the sort often seen round the neck of Dylan imitators, but it's certainly feasible, if complicated.

Wind instruments in general are tricky; percussion instruments, too, have their problems. Mostly not to do with playing while singing, but more to do with their inherent limitations in terms of tone and tune. One song accompanied only by a mournful drum may be atmospheric and darkly dramatic. A whole set will have people reaching for the painkillers and/or the phone number of the Samaritans.

Which brings us to another important point about solo performing – light and shade. Dynamics, expression and pacing are thrown into sharp relief when it's just a single musician. If you're in a band you can vary your sound by getting the bass and drums to stop, making the guitarist step on some pedal or other, bringing in some keyboards, or any of a huge number of other possible arrangement tricks. When it's just you and an instrument you have to think harder.

Yes, if you're playing something touch-sensitive you can play harder or more softly, and a single voice is capable of huge variations in tone and volume, but if you're playing more than one song the limitations in your instrumental capability come into play. The last thing you want to do is bore your audience; you're an easy target for their rotten veg if there's only one of you.

Speed is one factor: making sure there's enough variation between the slow songs and faster ones, and being smart about placing them in a set, will help a lot. Trying to use your whole range of dynamics from quiet to loud works. Keeping your set varied, if you're covering other people's material, is important. A whole set of, say, David Bowie's 'Laughing Gnome' period songs may not be a terribly good idea. If you're dead keen on Bowie, just adding a bit of Ziggy Stardust and some Station to Station would help add a different flavour.

But varying your instrumentation is a fine idea too. Yes, it's more things to carry, but if you watch almost any of the legendary solo artists they will swap between accompanying instruments all the time. Neil Young's solo sets, for instance, are performed in the middle of a music shop's worth of kit, from 6- and 12-string guitars to banjos, pump organs and pianos, from which he picks and chooses whatever works best with each song.

If you've never performed solo, you should. It's an adrenalin rush more extreme than anything short of bungee-jumping, and the sense of relief and satisfaction when you've managed to get through a whole set on your own without messing up, particularly if people actually clapped, is enormous. Like bungee-jumping, the worst bit is letting go and making the initial decision to do it, and also like bungee-jumping, it's extremely addictive. But you don't have to get hoisted up on a crane first. Unless you think it'll improve your set, of course.

JAMS AND OPEN MIC NIGHTS

Joining a band can be like a marriage – secure, yes, but sometimes a bumpy ride, with all its tiffs, responsibilities and long-term resentments. Being a solo artist is undeniably freer and demands far less commitment, but can sometimes feel like a rather lonely path.

So here's the musical alternative to both of those extremes. But what is its relationship equivalent? Swinging? An open relationship? Polygamy? A series of one-night stands? Maybe we'd better leave this analogy behind and move swiftly on before trouble starts...

If you're keen to play with other musicians but haven't got the time, or desire, to make a long-term commitment to a band, there's a sizeable network of jams and open mic nights that will allow you to get out of an evening, hop up on stage for a few numbers, then watch other people doing the same thing.

Venues that have bands on will often stage a jam or open mic night as a good way to bring in some people and sell some beer early in the week when it would otherwise be quiet. There's a wide range to suit most tastes and talents, from blues and folk to jazz and soul, and they go from fearsomely technical exercises in showing off your well-honed chops to relaxed ambles through easy old favourites, with rank amateurs encouraged.

If there's somebody you've thought about collaborating with musically, it's a good opportunity to rehearse and play a couple of numbers together to see if there's some synergy there. There's very little commitment required, either in time or effort.

You might be between bands, or otherwise having a layoff, and fancy a bit of playing just to brush the cobwebs away. Maybe you've got a few new numbers or even a new instrument to try out; doing it in front of a fairly benign and non-judgemental audience is a good test, with enough adrenalin to keep you on your toes and sharpen you up.

Some sessions can be quite serious, with a promoter hand-picking a selection of up-and-coming acts, or a hardcore of session musicians taking most of the slots, so make sure you know what you're getting into if you fancy having a go. By far the best way of doing this, of course, is to go along for an evening, without an instrument, preferably with a mate or two, and suss it out. No pressure; just see if it's the sort of thing you fancy and enjoy the music. They rarely cost much to get in, so it's a cheap evening out.

If you do think it's the sort of thing you'd like to have a go at, it's worth having a quick word with the organiser and checking what your chances are in the following weeks. The organiser will usually be a harassed-looking person with a clipboard hovering somewhere between the mixing desk, the stage and the bar; if you're in any doubt ask one of the musicians to point you in their direction. Open mic nights and popular folk club singers' nights tend to book up in advance; straightforward jams will be open to all-comers on the night, so it's worth finding out what the form is.

If you're contemplating going to a routine jam session – blues is a very fertile area for these – make sure you've brushed up on a few old favourites first.

START ME UP

Obviously you'll need to know the classic blues 12-bar pattern, but it's also worth learning a couple of solos – maybe a fast one and a slow one – as you're likely to get the opportunity to step out and solo if you're a guitar player, keyboardist, harp-blower or other front-line instrumentalist. If you're a drummer or bass player you're less likely to get a solo, but on the other hand rhythm section players always seem to be in demand so you'll probably get plenty of time on stage anyway. If you sing a bit and are happy to lead a band of strangers through a few numbers, you'll be much appreciated; again. there always seems to be a shortage of bandleaders.

If you're heading for a jazz session, the classic songbook is your friend; nobody necessarily wants to hear six versions of 'Sweet Georgia Brown', but at least the standards are something most players have in common, which short-cuts the tricky business of learning a new song on stage in 35 seconds flat.

Folk and singer-songwriter nights are more variable; that's why it's well worth going along on a reconnaissance mission first, so you can see if there's a house style or direction, and whether most people are tackling traditional songs or showcasing their own material.

There's another good reason for attending one of these musical free-for-alls, which is networking. Yes, that's a rubbish phrase scraped out of the bottom of the big-business bin, but you know what it means – making new musical contacts and friends, finding out what's going on and who's around, catching up on the gossip and maybe sharing some of your own.

There are many, many bands who've formed after meeting at a jam or open mic, and it's also a good way to learn about opportunities or important changes. Is a new venue opening? Is that place you're booked at in a month's time about to close down? Is a big band coming to town who might need a support act? Has your drummer/singer/whatever been spotted playing with another band? There's no better place to find out.

Of course, if you're already an established player with a wide circle of contacts and an enthusiasm for one type of music, you can go further than just turning up at a jam – you can run one. It might make you some pocket money, it's a good way to keep in touch with all those other musicians and it'll elevate your status on the local scene to demi-god (or at least demi-demi-god). If you're the organised type it's worth thinking about. Many venues would be very happy to fill those underused evenings early in the week, and if there's one thing musicians know how to do it's drink so if you manage to get a good crowd in, their increased bar takings will make you very popular. It's a fair amount of work, particularly ensuring that flaky but essential people actually turn up, but it can be rewarding and useful; if your own band gets to open and/or close the night, as is often the case, you get valuable exposure to a very well-connected audience.

But that's quite enough about commitment. Surely the point is to turn up out of the blue, amaze everybody with your incredible talent, then disappear into the night, leaving them wondering, 'Who was that masked musician?' Well, either that or badly fumble your way through something easy, then leave knowing full well that nobody's going to remember by this time next week. Either is good.

SPARE BEDROOM STYLE

So you don't fancy joining a band. Or forming one. Too much hassle, too much man-management. But playing solo isn't really getting your juices flowing either. Bit scary. Or just a bit boring. Jams? Open mic nights? Nah.

But you still want to do something. That musical itch is still there, demanding to be scratched. But how?

Performance isn't the be-all and end-all of playing. It can be a nice thing to do, if you're in the right frame of mind and have the ideal sort of material, but at its worst it can also be a real royal pain in the backside; a huge amount of work, money and rehearsal time for nothing more than an indifferent night out and a day's ear-ringing headache.

The aim, after all, isn't stardom. Not when you get past about 23 it isn't. It's enjoyment. So if something doesn't float your boat, don't do it. Simple as that.

And enjoyment can come from many directions. Like an involving, good-sounding solo recording session; a noticeable improvement in skill and technique on your instrument; or a clever, well-written song that stands comparison with your heroes'.

None of these, you'll notice, necessitate spending any time in a sweaty, noisy room full of beery, shouty people (whether that's your audience or your band). If you have little need for the affirmation and approval of a load of strangers, why bother gigging? Nobody's forcing you.

In all of those cases above, though, you need a space to call your own where you can concentrate, relax and be at your most productive. Hence the spare bedroom. It doesn't have to be literally that, of course; got a cellar or basement? An attic? A conservatory? A garage or shed? Indeed a corner of the kitchen or dining room can work.

Even if space is tight, how about time? Yes, that does sound a bit Dr Who, but here's the plan: find yourself a slot, ideally at a regular time (and also ideally coinciding with your Significant Other off doing something else) and stick to that as your playing/practising/recording time. Once you're in the groove, you'll get pretty swift at dragging your kit out of whatever dark cupboard it normally lurks in and setting it up. Of course, the perfect solution would be a purpose-built music room with everything plugged in and ready for instant use all the time, but life's not usually that perfect. If you can somehow achieve that, though, well done. Now all you have to do is find the time to actually go in there and use it, which is often the tricky bit.

There's quite a bit more on the practicalities of home recording, gear, sheds and other relevant matters further on in this book, but the only thing you really need to do is make sure you keep doing something musical, whether your home facilities include a fully soundproofed 64-track digital studio or just the odd half-hour on the sofa. Find a space, find some time and lose yourself in it for a bit.

CHAPTER 4

IN WITH THE IN CROWD

If you read that last chapter you'll have some idea about the pros and cons of joining bands, playing solo, or just sticking with home recording and practice.

If you haven't got to that bit yet, you're holding the book upside down. Try turning it round. That's better.

But while all of the approaches to music are equally valid (whatever floats your boat), there's a fair bit more to be said about the most mainstream and quite possibly the most popular of these: being in a band.

Although it's quite possible to get a lot of enjoyment out of music without any other people involved at all, many would argue that the social element is at least half the fun. Whether they'd still argue that after a week in a small van with a curry-addicted drummer is quite another matter, but it's certainly true that the interplay between musicians, both personally and while playing, adds another dimension to the whole experience. Man.

But it might have been a long while since you were in a band. Or you might never have been in one at all. Or perhaps you've just left one, or maybe you're starting to think that your solo efforts need a little more backup. Where do you start?

Well here, hopefully, are a set of tips, pointers and

other odds and sods of vaguely useful information to help you get together with a bunch of like-minded players in a musical ensemble.

And there are also a few hints on staying together without killing each other, committing multiple adultery (unless you're in a Fleetwood Mac tribute band, of course), or letting the whole thing turn into a terrible chore rather than the friendly and fun exercise that it should be.

In the end, it's all about getting on with a bunch of people who you might only have one thing in common with – music. It's about politics, man-management, diplomacy, logistics and communication. And if that all sounds a bit like the sort of stuff you have to do in boring meetings at work, then you're quite right – it is. Which is why having a bit of experience in those situations comes in very handy.

While bands of callow youths are flying off the handle, having meltdowns, hating each other, loving each other and veering wildly between despair and hysteria without ever really knowing why, us rather more experienced and worldly-wise types will have seen it all before. Understanding when to delegate and when to lead, recognising who the troublemakers are and how to defuse their antics, knowing how to offer well-earned praise and how to disagree without offending – these are all skills picked up in a working life, and those you'll need to be in a decent, enjoyable group.

Being in a band is not as dull and worky as that sounds, of course. It still involves visits to the pub and, naturally, making some fine music. But it's not quite as simple as you might think. So here's how it works...

IN WITH THE IN CROWD

CHOOSING A GENRE

Nobody likes everything. It's impossible. Whether it's broccoli, dentists or Jeremy Clarkson's trousers, there's always something you hate, something that sets your teeth on edge and gives you a quick involuntary shudder.

And conversely, there must be something that you adore above all else. It's unlikely to be Jeremy Clarkson's trousers (unless you're Mrs Clarkson) but there's something out there that makes you come over all unnecessary and gives you a bit of a warm glow inside.

Those two, Things You Love and Things You Hate, are the ends of the spectrum. In between comes everything else, dotted along an invisible line through 'quite like' and 'not bad' via 'all right, I suppose' and 'don't mind it'.

And that's what you'll have to wrestle with when you're deciding what sort of band you'd like to join or form. And what's more, you'll have to think about it from two different angles. When you're considering the music you appreciate, it's not just what sort of music you enjoy listening to, it's also what type of music you'd take pleasure in playing.

These two things are by no means the same. Like sport, for instance, where playing a few games of pool might be huge fun, but watching the World Snooker Championships is like a double dose of Valium; you might also enjoy riding your bike to the shops, but you may well not care *un peu* about the Tour de France. That difference between spectating and participating is exactly the same in music.

So think about what's in your record collection or on your iPod, but don't restrict yourself purely to that. In many cases learning a brand new set of riffs or techniques is very satisfying, and playing something that's a little outside your musical comfort zone is an excellent discipline to broaden your musical horizons and improve your technique.

For instance, if you mainly listen to classic rock, how about going back to its roots and trying some straight blues? Or if you're a jazz cat, why not try adding some improvisational style to a soul band? If you're a huge fan of one particular band, take a listen to some of their side projects and creative excursions into other musical areas. Even the biggest bands almost always tinker about with things that are outside their usual sphere, to mixed but often interesting effect.

It'll start off as an intriguing experiment, but before you know it you'll have started to build up a knowledge of, and probably even a liking for, a whole new genre.

And then there the practicalities. If you play piccolo flute, no matter how keen you may be, you're unlikely to get a gig with a Ramones tribute band. And trombonists rarely feature with fey, sensitive acoustic singer-songwriters (though I'd pay good money to hear that).

Where you live will have a bearing on your choices too. If you're somewhere deeply rural, there may well be a strong folk scene but roots reggae may not be on the agenda. Conversely, if you're in somewhere urban and achingly hip, you might find you'll have to travel out of town to find anything other than 14-year-old hipsters with comedy glasses and bumfluff beards.

So be practical, be flexible and be prepared to fruitlessly kiss a few frogs before you find a band that you can work with, and whose music you are at least prepared to try playing.

Of course, you already know where on that spectrum of likes and dislikes most genres sit; or you think you do. Blues? It's for old farts with croaky voices. Jazz? It's for old farts with stupid hats. Rock? It's for old farts with embarrassing trousers. Folk? It's for old farts with pewter tankards of real ale. Etc etc.

But once you're enjoying playing with some pleasant, competent musicians you may find that even if you start off not particularly liking their chosen style of music, you'll warm to it and hopefully be able to contribute something a little different. After all, if everybody in a band had exactly the same influences it would be a very dull world indeed.

If you're looking for a new musician, or forming a band, exactly the same thing applies. When a potential new recruit turns up and reels off a set of influences and previous bands which aren't the same as yours, it's all too tempting to think 'Oh, they'll never fit in' and bid them a polite goodbye.

But hang on a minute. Put their current tastes to one side and think. Are they nice people? Are they flexible and willing to learn? Do they have anything they can teach you? Would it be worth trying them out, just to see if there is any common ground, now or potentially after a few more rehearsals?

Or maybe, if you're both dead set on different directions and totally unwilling to compromise, it'll never work. That's possible. But again, if there's any shadow of a doubt give it a go. Be clear that it's a trial run, but what have you got to lose? Your death metal/ doom rock ensemble may be vastly improved with the addition of some folk concertina or a bit of country pedal steel. Maybe...

COVERS OR ORIGINALS?

When you're thinking about joining or forming a band, it's always worth considering your future aims and ambitions. Obviously, be realistic. That headlining slot at Glastonbury may take a few months to achieve. A sold-out global stadium tour could take even longer. A private jet and your own custom-built studio on a Caribbean island? Could be a job for next year. Difficult to believe it'll take that long, isn't it?

When you wake up, however, you'll need to set your sights a little lower and mull over a rather less grandiose set of ambitions.

For instance, do you enjoy gigging? Do you want to play to more than a few friends, earn a bit of money to offset expenses and play reasonable venues fairly often?

Or maybe you're just in it for the music – a few laughs, some rehearsals, occasional songwriting sessions and the chance to play your own material to a select but appreciative audience. Obviously both would be nice, but let's be sensible for a moment.

If the first route seems more appealing, you're far likelier to achieve that sort of thing by playing cover versions: other people's (usually well-known) songs – either as a 'tribute' band to a particular artist, a specialist act covering a narrow spectrum of styles, or an all-purpose bar band bashing out a set of guaranteed crowd-pleasers.

If the second alternative is more your bag, original material is probably the way to go. It's more challenging, both for band and audience, but more satisfying in many ways if it works.

This doesn't necessarily have to be an either/or; some bands leaven their own songs with a sprinkling of better-known material from other artists, and even the biggest bands will sometimes sneak a cover version or two into their set. REM, for instance, were well known, even during their impenetrably arty indie-rock phase, for throwing in deeply unlikely cover versions like Roger Miller's 'King of the Road' or Gloria Gaynor's 'I Will Survive'.

And there are certainly some bands who have subsidised their original material by sneaking out under a pseudonym and playing pop covers at working men's clubs and weddings. There aren't many who will admit it, but more than a few highly credible indie stars have a sparkly shirt and a well-worn copy of the music to 'Mustang Sally' hiding at the back of the wardrobe.

Why is this? Well, audiences are funny things. Outside of the keen, hip and adventurous few they mostly want stuff they've already heard, done in the style of the original. They don't want a band so much as a live jukebox they can shout at. This can be desperately dispiriting for original artists, who spend a fair bit of their time trying to get people to listen to their own material, the fruits of their own hard labour and creative inspiration, when all the crowd actually wants is a cover version of 'Knock On Wood'.

And the paid covers circuit, particularly in social clubs, can be a tough, no-nonsense place. It's difficult to feel like a rock superstar when you're definitely playing second on the bill to the bingo, and you're sharing a tiny dressing room with a stroppy magician whose rabbit has just pooped in your guitar case. But if you decide that cover versions are the way to go, whether that's due to wanting reliable gigs, only enjoying one particular style of music, or just not being bothered about trying to write originals, there are still a wide range of choices.

If you're technically skilled, really focused on the technique of one artist or just a huge fan of a band, forming or joining a tribute band is nowadays a good route to regular, paid gigs. There's a well-developed circuit, with the better acts being able to earn a decent living and play some good-sized venues. Acts like The Australian Pink Floyd, The Bootleg Beatles and Björn Again, to name just a few, have capitalised on those acts who have given up touring due to lawsuits, disillusionment and/or death and are presenting a pretty decent facsimile of their subjects' sound to fans who are happy to accept a faithful copy, as the originals are no longer available.

This is not easy, mind you. You have to get it absolutely right or the audience will, quite justifiably, feel they've been diddled. This may mean buying the same gear as the musician you're copying, wearing the same stage gear and even trying to get as close to their light show as possible on a limited budget. This is not as easy as even that sounds. Doing The Beatles? You'll need a left-handed bass player who can sing lead. Pink Floyd? Be prepared to spend a lot of time learning how to get those distinctive, technically complex sounds. In fact anybody who's tackling progressive rock with its capes, puppets, flying pigs, banks of synthesisers, lasers and ultra-complicated song structures, deserves a round of applause. In 7/4 time, with two bars of 9/8, while wearing a long wig.

But if you don't want to take cover versions to that extreme then you can still put together a more mixed, more casual set that'll keep people entertained and hopefully get you booked at some decent places. Some bands concentrate on a particular era or style – '70s soul or funk, for instance, or '60s rhythm and blues, are popular choices, but anything from big reggae hits to New Orleans blues, art-rock to synth-pop has its audience. If there's a selection of popular songs that flow together as a set and get people moving some part of their body, chances are there'll be a band somewhere in the world that's playing them.

Of course, it's worth mentioning that there are some genres that don't just tolerate cover versions but positively invite them. While folk music has its share of genius songwriters, many of its classic songs have been handed down from generation to generation for every player or singer to put their own stamp on. Hoary old chestnuts like 'John Barleycorn', 'Reynardine' and 'Green Grow the Rushes, O' may be centuries old, but that doesn't mean that today's minstrels can't give them a tweak and revitalise them yet again.

Blues and jazz, too, have their own set of classics which are trotted out endlessly for reinterpretation and rearrangement without, it seems, audiences getting bored with them. (Or at least when they're played only once a night. Some blues jam sessions can feature at least three versions of 'I'm a Man', 'Little Red Rooster' or 'Smokestack Lightning', which can get more than a tad tedious.)

But if you fancy putting together a set of reliable, low-maintenance crowd-pleasing classics, you could do a lot worse than going to see some of the local bands who are doing exactly that. Which of their songs go down especially well? And which ones go down like a, er, Led Zeppelin? Because, you see, when you're playing covers to a paying crowd it's not about you and your desperate wish to recreate side four of *Physical Graffiti* note for note; it's all about what the punters want to hear. While you're checking out the potential opposition, also have a think about what they're playing – and what they're not. Is there a gap for a different kind of band? If they're all very similar, is there a good reason for that, or could you offer an interesting alternative?

It all sounds a bit cold-blooded and businesslike. Market research? It'll be focus groups and online surveys next. But if you're intending to go out and entertain people, while earning a reasonable sum, you've got to be smart. It's a serious business, letting people have fun.

Though once you've got your band together and your set worked out, you do get to play some tremendous songs to a bunch of folk who are determined to have a really excellent time. It's difficult not to enjoy that bit; a good sweaty gig to an appreciative, lively audience, followed by a reasonable lump of payment, is well worth doing a bit of homework first.

But what if that doesn't appeal to you? What if the idea of playing a bunch of classic pop songs to some mildly drunken revellers every Friday and Saturday gives you sense of deep and overwhelming existential ennui?

Don't despair; writing and performing your own songs is still a very viable option. Just don't expect it to be as well rewarded financially or as straightforward when it comes to booking local gigs. However, you may well be happy to swap a bit more hassle for a lot more creative freedom.

If songwriting is an itch that just has to be scratched – and playing other people's songs can certainly be more than a bit tedious after what feels like your 5,000th rendition of 'Honky Tonk Women' or 'Can't Get You Out Of My Head' – then putting together a band that has a distinctive sound, playing material that you've created and crafted, and winning over an audience with your own songs, is about as satisfying as it gets.

That also opens up the areas of recording and even releasing your own material; while cover versions may be a fun live event, they're rarely worth the bother of going into the studio to record, as someone else has already done that, and probably better.

So you pays your money – or earns your money – and takes your choice. Originals? Covers? Bit of both?

FRIENDS

There is, of course, another way to get a band together, or join one, other than placing or answering an ad. This way, however, is fraught with potential perils, and can have awful effects on your social life, your non-musical activities and even your relationship. Consider yourself warned. Now will you take the red pill or the blue pill?

That hard and dangerous way is, in fact, getting together with your friends. Do you have a mate or two who also play? Are they seeking a new musician, or are you looking for something that they do? Before you think 'Oh, that's an easy option', though, think long and hard.

The problem with getting into a band with old friends is that while you may get along extremely well with them in the pub or at a dinner party, you're dealing with a whole different set of manners and stresses when you're trying to make music.

That charming person with the lovely partner and the cheerful kids might turn into an ego-driven, wilful, incompetent or otherwise annoying horror when they strap on a guitar, get behind a drum kit or plug in a microphone.

And the major drawback of that, of course, is that when or if you fall out with them badly over a drum fill or a guitar solo, a missed gig or a superstar tantrum, you can kiss goodbye to the rest of your social contacts. Is your partner best friends with theirs? Ooh, tricky. Are you both locals at the same pub? One of you might have to rethink that. And so on.

Naturally, playing in a band with mates can be great fun. And if you're all grown-up enough or relaxed enough to work out or laugh off any conflicts, that's excellent. But it's not worth losing friends just for the sake of playing a few notes. Try to remember that if you suddenly think 'Hang on, doesn't so-and-so from the pub play a bit of bass...?'

By the way, this also goes for close colleagues at work. And don't even think about sharing a stage with your boss. This will almost certainly not end well, however laid back their management style.

ADS

If you're thinking of joining a band, forming a band, or just hunting for a new member, unless your local contacts are excellent and word of mouth alone does the job, you'll have to get involved in the world of advertising.

Sadly, this doesn't involve wearing a sharp suit, drinking gallons of dry martini and having a slinky secretary, whatever *Mad Men* might suggest.

Instead, it usually means one of two things, depending on whether you're looking to join up or searching for recruits.

One is putting a small ad somewhere you hope other like-minded musicians will spot it, and wording said advert in a way that, firstly, will attract exactly the sort of people you're after, secondly, will sum up what exactly it is you're trying to do and, thirdly, will make you sound wise, intelligent and reliable. Harder than it sounds, then. Maybe you will need that dry martini after all.

The other is finding and reading other people's ads, and interpreting their sometimes horribly confusing language so you don't get the wrong end of the stick and accidentally join an extreme death metal act when you were looking for a traditional folk group. Or, more likely, waste everybody's time at a slightly embarrassing and fruitless audition.

Where to look? These days, mostly online. There are quite a few websites that claim to be the best place to find band and musicians – there's a fairly complete list in the facty bit at the back of this book. Some ask you to register, some ask for money, some want neither, but there's no stand-out market leader at the moment.

Or there's classified site Gumtree (not bad), its old-established rival Loot (fairly poor), your local paper (unlikely to be much use), or just a bit of paper stuck on a board at your neighbourhood music shop, rehearsal studio or gig venue (often surprisingly effective). In that last case, make sure you include a few rip-offable slips with contact details, plus a reminder of what they're for, at the bottom. Something like 'Bassist for reggae band – call [number] or email [address]'. Many musicians have enough trouble remembering their guitar and amp let alone a pen and paper, so make it easy for them.

So let's assume that you're forming a band or seeking a replacement musician. Before you begin writing that ad, get your ideas straight. What, exactly, are you looking for? No, not just 'somebody who isn't that last idiot we had to sack'. What sort of person would fit? What sound are you aiming for?

If you're forming or running a band, be clear about your aims and your schedule. Are you intending to tour and record profusely, or are you just up for a weekly rehearsal and the occasional gig? Are you in it for the money, the musical satisfaction or the beer? Be plain about this. It's sad when a perfectly fine player doesn't fit because their ambition or level of commitment isn't the same as yours.

Next, where are you based, and how willing to travel

are you? Do you have a permanent rehearsal room, or are you relying on one-off sessions? That's important. Carting gear is a huge hassle for some people (we're looking at you, double bass players and Hammond organists).

And how old are you or your band? Don't forget this. A herd of squeaky teenagers won't want some wrinkly old duffer turning up, no matter how skilled, and you will almost certainly not share a set of influences with a youngster, no matter how keen, who was born well after the first Radiohead album came out.

And then the $64,000 dollar question – what are your influences? This is where most people get it horribly wrong by listing every band they've ever heard of in a confusing and unreadable directory, or going completely the other way and just saying 'rock'.

What you're trying to do is give a concise, if necessarily rough, guide to how you sound or how you'd like to sound. It's a good exercise anyway, because when you're on the phone to a promoter or landlord, they won't have a spare 20 minutes for you to wibble on about a load of obscure bands either. Get your ideas straight on who your major influences are and it'll help with all sorts of things, including song selection, set lists and posters.

So, no more than three or four bands or artists. Keep it simple. And include a detailed genre if possible. For instance: 'Chicago Blues band – Muddy Waters, Little Walter, Howlin' Wolf...' or 'English folk guitarist – Bert Jansch, Martin Carthy, Richard Thompson...'.

Yes, of course your influences are more varied, interesting and cosmopolitan than that, but this is not the time to go into that level of detail. By all means use words like 'eclectic' or 'varied' but don't confuse people. Give them some simple signposts, then give them the bigger picture when, or if, you meet in person. And don't show off. This isn't a chance to boast about the breadth of your record collection, it's an attempt to find as many roughly like-minded candidates as possible.

Also, spelling and grammar. Or, as many ads would have it, speling and gramer. For goodness sake spell-check your ad or you look like an idiot. Write it in something like Microsoft Word that has a built-in spell-checker first, then copy and paste it into your chosen ad website's text box (it's almost always a website these days, but most don't offer spellchecking). And use normal case rather than ALL CAPITALS, which makes you sound a bit shouty. iF yOR iN A PuNK baND OfF cAWsE iGNaW ThIsS.

Don't get too literary or long-winded. Keep it simple, clear and easy to understand. A 1,500 word essay on your entire musical journey to date, complete with explanatory footnotes and short biographies of all members current and past might be fun to write, but it'll be a slog to read.

However, there's nothing to stop you injecting a little salesmanship. It never hurts to mention 'gigs booked' or 'good contacts' or 'own rehearsal room'. Provided you do, of course, have these things. Blatant lying rarely ends well. If there's one thing drummers do well, it's hitting things. Bear that in mind.

You don't need to start with 'Hi!', 'Hello!' or 'Howdy' (even if you're a C&W band). It's not a letter or an email, it's a bit of advertising. Do British Airways start their TV commercials with 'Hi there, dudes and dudettes!!!'? No.

Do you have a good photo of the band, or a video? Do they show you off to great advantage, without making a player you're trying to replace look like an unmatchable hero? If so, good. Use them. If you're not sure, though, don't. A mildly embarrassing group shot or a wobbly, muffled video will put off more people than it attracts. If in doubt, don't.

Also, try to keep it professional. Yes, you may have a huge and vengeful hatred of the person you've just fired for stealing your gear, failing to turn up to your gigs and sleeping with your girlfriend/boyfriend/dog. But this is not the time to exorcise those demons. Don't use this ad as a public pulpit to rant from. This will make people assume that you are a bitter, twisted nutcase. Which may be true, but there's no need to make it too obvious.

And lastly, keep your contact details simple too. A band email is handy, or one reliable member's mobile. But all too often you get 'call Jeremy on 079768 8282839 on Fridays between 2 and 4pm, or if no answer call Frank's wife on 08674 2877790 and leave a message, or if that doesn't ring because she's locked in the basement try Geoff on 095874 526735 after midnight on every other Wednesday' Make it straightforward and easy to get in touch. It'll also make you look organised and efficient, which is a big plus point.

So what if you're on the other side of the fence, and are browsing ads to find a band? Well, first, read the above and see if the ads you're looking at meet all those criteria. If so, that's very hopeful – you may have found one of the few organised, sensible and totally honest bands on the planet. Well done. Get in touch fast, as they'll have a bit of a queue.

But it's unlikely. So how do you decode the various scrambled messages?

The first step is to decide what you want. Are you just up for a bit of occasional fun, or are you keen on more regular commitments? Paid or hobby? Do you have a cast-iron desire to play one particular kind of music, or are you adaptable on style and genre?

Try to filter the ads you're looking at by all those things, but don't be too fixed. Flexibility is vital because you're only getting a brief snapshot rather than the whole picture. If there's even a faint spark of interest, it's worth getting in touch and exploring further. If you enjoy, say, modern country and a band mentions '70s soft rock, it's worth seeing if there's any common ground there. They might be very happy to veer towards The Eagles, Manassas and Gram Parsons and give Supertramp and ELO the elbow.

Don't forget that if you become a member of a band you'll usually get a vote in their direction (unless they're run by a total fascist, but that's something you'll usually only find out when you meet up. Swastika armbands are often a clue).

When you answer an ad, if it's by email, keep in mind all of the above advice – be concise, be organised and try not to sound like a dimwit.

You only need to get them interested enough to meet up because that first meeting, whether a chat over a pint or a formal audition, is where you'll really find out in depth what they're like and where they're going musically. List a few similar or complementary influences to their own, describe your style in as straightforward a way as possible, maybe mention your gear if it's of a decent standard, and don't forget a few personal details such as where you live, if you have transport, your age and any relevant previous experience.

Starting to sound like a job application? Too right. That's basically what it is at first – the beer, laughs and friendly banter comes later, if you get over the first, wary, formal, contact. So make yourself sound organised and competent; unless you're applying to join Kolonel Kooky's Komedy Kapers save the wacky sense of humour for later.

But what if all your browsing comes up blank? Then it's time to post your own ad. Again, be absolutely clear about what you want but don't sound too demanding. There's a fantastic spoof ad floating around, mostly on American ad site Craigslist, which is worth quoting in full, not just because it's funny but because it's all too accurate:

"Bass player available for PAYING GIGS ONLY. I play G, C, D. If your songs are not in G, please transpose them into G. If your song has an Em or Bm or anything off the wall I will probably sit out that chord. Or I could learn those notes for $30 each. If you want me to do fancy stuff like go back and forth between G and D while you hold a G chord, forget it because I'm a 'pocket' player.

"Minimum $100 per gig within a 5 mile radius of my home. $5 per mile travel charge for other areas out of town. Please make sure your gigs are on a local bus route, or you can pick me up at my place. Must be home by 11pm due to previous legal hassles. No gigs within 500 yards of schools, parks, or playgrounds."

Very amusing indeed. But anyone who reads musicians' ads regularly will recognise that all-too-real combination of demanding, self-centred and dim. Also, the criminal background thing. That too.

Don't sound like that. So you think you're a fantastic player. Don't bang on about it, bighead. So you can't do Mondays or Wednesdays. Don't make a big deal out of it. So you haven't got a car. Something can usually be arranged.

In short, accentuate the positives; make yourself sound like the kind of smart, sensible and accommodating person that anyone would be delighted to have in their band. That first face-to-face meeting with your potential bandmates is the time to start discussing the details – an advert is just a way to get to that point.

If it doesn't work the first time, though, keep trying. Try other sites and more places. And experiment with changing your ad. Doing a short, concise one? Add in a few more details. A bit lengthy? Give it a cut. And don't forget that not everybody checks the ads every day, so make sure you give it a good run and re-post several times.

Many websites, like Gumtree, can get so busy that your ad can slide down the rankings pretty fast, so make sure you post it at a popular time of day like early evening – if you put it on at 8.30am it'll be halfway down page 17 by the time people get home from work and turn on their laptops.

So good luck with the advertising campaign. May you find a perfect musician or a great band quickly and painlessly. And if you do, maybe you should consider a career as a copywriter. Apparently there are a lot of martinis involved...

AUDITIONS

So there you are, wandering into an unfamiliar room in a dodgy part of town to be met by a set of strangers eyeing you up in a highly critical, if not rather threatening, way. Is it a mugging? A gangland ambush? No, it's an audition.

If you're thinking of joining a band, this will often be your way in – or not. And if you're putting a band together, this may be your preferred way of checking out potential players.

Auditions, however, can often be an unpleasant chore for all concerned – and may well not even be the best way of showing off or assessing suitability and talent. But they do have their uses (not least frightening sensitive musicians silly). So how do you make them useful and relatively painless?

As a would-be band member, it goes like this. Let's say you've answered a small ad or replied to a notice in the local music shop. After a short email conversation or phone call, you're told we're holding auditions for the post on such-and-such a date and time; see you there. Auditions are pretty much par for the course in some styles of music: classical ensembles, big bands and stars' backing groups all like to assess your technical ability pretty thoroughly before they hire you. The more successful and profitable a band is, whether that's a tribute act, a club circuit outfit or a relatively well-known set-up, the more likely they are to require a formal audition process. Like any job, the longer the queue of potential recruits, the more hoops they feel able to make you jump through.

But if you're just thinking of joining a bunch of amateurs round the corner, and you're pretty sure you're the only applicant, it seems a bit excessive, if not egotistical.

Another problem with auditions is that you arrive, set up your gear, play a few numbers, have a very brief conversation, because the band are usually paying for studio time, and leave. This is a fine way to answer just one question, which is 'How good are you at impressing people with your technical proficiency while under extreme pressure?' It doesn't, however, deal with any of the many other aspects of having an enjoyable and creative long-term musical relationship. We all know somebody who is highly skilled but in all other ways a waste of valuable oxygen, with the social skills of a cane toad and the morals of a hyena. An audition is a perfect method for a band to hire exactly that person, then wonder why they're not having much fun any more.

There are plenty of other rather less nerve-wracking ways to start a musical relationship. Meeting for a no-commitment chat, for instance. This, whether it's over a coffee, a beer, or just a natter in the local music shop or rehearsal room, can be a very good way to compare influences, styles, ambitions and availability. It doesn't matter if it's with the entire band, a couple of key members or just the bandleader, it's a good way to assess the mutual fit and iron out a few of the more practical elements of any potential hook-up.

This will certainly make a subsequent audition more friendly and productive; you'll have met before, so will all be able to relax a bit, and it's also a good way of weeding out those players who are a poor creative match, have time or distance issues, or are just idiots.

It works the other way round, too; as a would-be recruit you get the chance to assess the band dynamics, pick out the funny one and the morose one and see whether they're going to be fun, busy and involving or are just a bunch of bedroom dreamers who will spend the next 15 years contemplating playing their first gig but never quite getting it together.

So let's say that first hurdle has been overcome and it's all looking quite positive. Now it's time to turn up and show off your stuff (or conversely wait for your victims – sorry, potential musicians – to do just that).

If you're auditioning, be well practised, on time and organised. Don't just pick up your instrument, blow a thick layer of dust off it and saunter along; make sure you're on top form and if you've been asked to learn a song or two, make doubly sure that you've got it all committed to memory. And double-check all keys, if not mentioned. Suddenly having to transpose a song you've learned in D into Bb is a good way to make even the best musician look like a bit of a berk.

Check out where you're going well before time so you can think about bus routes, train times or parking. Don't get lost. And don't be late. Sounds simple, but if you're going somewhere unfamiliar there may well be traps like devious one-way systems, multiple entrances or other transport hassle. Also, make sure your phone is charged and that you've got at least one contact number in case of emergencies.

Get your gear sorted out. Try not to take loads of kit, because taking 20 minutes to set it all up will be boring and stressful for all concerned. If an item is essential to your sound then by all means take it, but try to pare your set-up down to a highly portable but decent-sounding minimum.

Make sure it's all in perfect working order and all leads, connectors and plugs are present and correct. Take spares – strings, sticks, batteries, picks, whatever – just in case. A mid-audition breakdown leaves a pretty poor impression.

Another trick: learn a simple chord sequence or riff, either your own or from some suitable cover version, and practise playing over it; everything from a simple rhythm pattern to a scorching solo. It's fairly common that either as a warming-up exercise at the start of an audition, or at the end if you run out of pre-learned or familiar material, somebody will say, "Why don't we jam for a bit?" This sounds like a fine idea, but often there's a slightly uncomfortable silence while everyone racks their brains to think of a suitable basis for jamming. That's when you whip out your trump card and teach the band your chord sequence, thereby impressing everybody with your creativity, initiative and incredible musical talent. While failing to mention, of course, the fact that you've been practising this seemingly simple sequence for ages.

But what if you've decided to hold auditions for your band? The same things largely apply: be organised, be on time – don't let players overrun their time slots – and get the gear sorted out. Hire or borrow a fairly all-purpose amp or drum kit so they don't have to drag all their own gear along, and make sure you let them know this fact, so they can make that decision themselves.

Send out detailed, up-to-date directions, contact numbers and times. Watch out for web links; some studios are pretty poor at updating their websites, so double-check they've got all the right details on there.

If you're auditioning more than one candidate, keep your phone in plain view so if another would-be player calls, lost, late or confused, midway through a song, you can get back to them as soon as practical.

And make sure the rest of the band are sounding slick and professional. Remember, auditions are two-way affairs. You might come across the greatest player ever, but if they're unimpressed by the band's air of shambolic disorganisation and lacklustre sound you've lost them.

And lastly, try to make it fun. Stony-faced cool may seem like a great rock 'n' roll pose, but bear in mind that auditions are a tense affair and you'll find out more about a player's true talent or a band's real personality if you relax a bit and try to make the process enjoyable and friendly. Good luck...

REHEARSALS

Rehearsals can be fun. Note the word 'can'. Because for many, they're a necessary evil; a tedious chore, like fighting some particularly boring enemy in a long-winded computer game just so you can get to the next level.

Others, though, never progress beyond that stage and actually don't particularly want to. A regular rehearsal is enough for them, fulfilling the musical equivalent of taking the dog for a walk or riding your bicycle to the shops by being a little gentle exercise for the musical muscles, just enough to keep their creativity ticking over.

But in either case they can be unpleasant, boring and unproductive or they can be enjoyable, useful and interesting. It's all to do with how you approach them and what your end result is supposed to be.

The first thing to contemplate is frequency. How much rehearsal time is enough? Many busy gigging bands hardly ever rehearse, only meeting offstage occasionally to learn a new number or freshen up some arrangements. This can be fine if you're happy to play substantially the same set in the same way every time, or you have a huge number of songs learned perfectly and can pick and choose between them to keep your live set fresh. But it's still worth considering taking a few hours every so often to rework those old chestnuts that have dropped out of favour, or to integrate a few new songs or even new instruments into your sound.

For most, though, particularly when starting up a band or adding new members, rehearsals need to be a lot more frequent. Once a week is usual, but if commitments allow, it's a very good discipline to try and work them in more often for a spell. There's a reason that professional bands sound so slick – it's that they've been rehearsing for a solid chunk of time, often weeks long, before they go off on tour. They've rehearsed every move and every note until it's deeply ingrained and the band meshes together perfectly, and as they've been rehearsing every day there hasn't been time to lose track of any of the details.

The problem with infrequent rehearsals is that it's easy to forget half of what you did the previous time, so you end up in a 'two steps forward, one step back' scenario. Relearning the same stuff every week, or going over it again and again for the sake of one memory-addled member, is a good way to bore yourself silly with your own material.

So more is better, but even if finances and time allow plenty of rehearsal time, the second thing to consider is the quality of your rehearsals. There are two elements to this: one is the venue, and the other is up to you – it's discipline.

First, though, where do you rehearse? If it's a 'proper' rehearsal studio, that's probably a good thing in terms of facilities and ease of use; most of the gear's already there, so you don't have to fiddle around for hours setting up a PA, and you might even be able to leave your own kit in a storage facility there, so you don't have to cart anything but your instrument.

A swift sidetrack on the subject of rehearsal room gear storage, however – remember that while it's convenient it's almost always at your own risk, and that a few musicians or their hangers-on are light-fingered scumbags and will take any opportunity to sneak off with something small, valuable and/or unsecured. Just make absolutely sure that your gear is firmly locked away, not mixed with any other band's kit, and try not to leave anything too portable like pedals, bags of leads, and so on lying around. The vast majority of players are honest, but there's always the odd one or two...

Another possible problem with rehearsal studios is cost; it's not terribly cheap hiring a room, PA and any other bits like drums or amps, so it's tempting to cut down on rehearsals for budgetary reasons. This is a shame, as you'll take twice as long to get to the level you're aiming at.

There are other options, though, the most basic, cheap one being just to meet at somebody's house and thrash out material acoustically. This is fine if they live in a detached cottage 400 yards from the nearest inhabitant, but really not ideal if it's a flat in a large block with paper-thin walls and twitchy neighbours. If needs must, then unplugged electric guitars and a drummer using brushes on a telephone directory can bring noise levels down to an acceptable domestic level, and this may be fine for learning the basics of songs or arrangements. But it's not a long-term solution.

If you're lucky enough to have a large shed or garage, that's jolly fine. A good shed can be a great option; you get to leave your gear set up, the kettle's close by and you can come and go as you please. But bear in mind a few things. Firstly, sheds have very thin walls so some sound insulation (and heat insulation in winter) is a good idea. Secondly, bands take up a surprisingly large amount of room. Your shed may look big, but when you've got a PA, a drummer, some keyboards, amps, guitars and several people packed in there it can get a bit sardine-like. And thirdly, you have to be security-conscious if you're thinking of leaving valuable gear in somewhere secured by a small padlock and about half an inch of softwood door. Thefts from sheds (usually of tools, motorbikes, bicycles and other easily disposable items) are by no means uncommon, so think about beefing up security. There's a whole section on sheds later on in this book, so dash on to Chapter Seven if you want more shed-sorting secrets.

Then there's the option of a space that isn't actually a rehearsal room, but is available – a scout hut, village hall, community centre, school classroom, church, the function room at your local pub, or whatever. Almost always this will involve dragging everything you need, including a PA, in at the beginning, then clearing it all up neatly at the end. There may be furniture to shift, table-tennis tables or other sports equipment to wheel out of the way and other physical obstacles to overcome. There may also be noise issues if other people are using the place too; nothing ruins an old folks' tombola evening quite like a massively loud drummer and 200 watts of heavily distorted guitar solo blasting through the wall. Also, acoustics can be hit-and-miss. Not that professional studios are all flawless in this respect, but you'll often find when you turn the volume up a little that there'll be an irritating echo, boom or resonant ring. This can sometimes be sorted out by drawing curtains and moving absorbent furniture, but it can be a nuisance.

But if that's all sorted out, it'll usually be cheap and local, and offer plenty of usable space. If you're looking for this sort of place just ask around the local community, and if there's a nearby pub that has bands on don't forget to try them too – their venue may be going spare at other times of the week.

So you've found your space. What now? That's where the structure and discipline bit comes in. Ask yourself before every rehearsal, 'What are we trying to achieve tonight?' Because there's nothing more tedious than endless, boring directionless rehearsals. That'll break up a band faster than almost anything else.

So let's imagine an average rehearsal.

Everybody arrives, eventually, at different stages of lateness and with various unlikely excuses for said tardiness.

Gear is dragged out of storage or hauled out of cars. Leads are found, or not found and borrowed, and plugged in. Some don't work. The guitarist has one pedal that makes an amazingly irritating eeeeeeeee noise because it's broken.

Instruments are tuned, but only one person has remembered to bring a tuner, so this takes quite a while.

You're nearly ready to play something, but the singer's busy checking his hair in a mirror and the bass player's gone round to the shop to buy beer and there's a long queue.

He arrives with the beer, then almost immediately the drummer knocks a can flying with his elbow and it's gone all over the mixer so there's a scrabble for some loo roll to mop it up.

Then finally you're ready to do something useful, but nobody can decide what. Maybe that song that didn't quite work the other night? No, the keyboard player doesn't like that one because he doesn't get to play much on it, so it gets shelved. What about that new number we talked about? Oh hang on, the singer's forgotten his lyric sheet.

All of this, of course, is going on to a background of random twiddling at enormous volume. The drummer's going biddly-biddly-bish, biddly, ba-dum-tish-biddle. The guitarist's going widdly widdly widdly wah widdly weeeeee. The bass player's going ba-bump, boop, ba-bum. The keyboard player's going doink, doink, doink, doink. Even the singer's going 'one-two, one-two' while he fiddles with the PA.

It makes your head hurt even thinking about it, doesn't it? You're probably over an hour in by this point and nothing has been done at all, yet everybody's already a bit tetchy.

This is bad. This is not a good way to rehearse, yet it's all too common. So you have to have some rules and a bit of discipline. Yes, it's a hobby not a job, but it'll be a lot more enjoyable if you're a bit more organised.

So set some ground rules. Being on time is a good idea, and being on time with beer already purchased is even better. Make sure that all gear is in working order before the rehearsal, not when you get there. Get your kit out at home and test it, then make sure you have everything you need plus a few likely spares. And don't take tons of stuff you won't use; that's a waste of time and energy.

The time to play around with settings, sounds and solo technique is at home, not in a band rehearsal. If you're desperate to try something that can only be achieved at full stage volume, hire a small rehearsal room for yourself and try it out without deafening or boring everyone else.

And when you're not playing a song, SHUT UP. It's true that your only chance to hear your instrument at proper volume may be at rehearsals, but get there early, stay late or use the tip above if you like. But don't endlessly twiddle around. It's annoying and unnecessary. If you ever get the chance to watch a professional band rehearsing, that's one thing you'll notice – between songs is dead silence other than sensible conversation. If someone needs to work on their sound, they'll do it elsewhere, or ask everyone to take a quick break while they sort it out. This makes sense. It's not a knob-twiddling exercise, it's about learning how to play songs as well as you can. So stay focused on that bit, not techy fiddling or random bashing about.

It always helps to have a plan. And that makes perfect sense for rehearsals, just as much as for bank jobs or zombie attacks. What are you trying to achieve? Which bits of your current repertoire need work, and what? How many new songs should you try to learn, and to what degree of proficiency? Do you need to work on backing vocals, or instrumental interplay, or starts and stops?

And set reasonable targets. If you try to learn 12 new songs in 3 hours you won't be able to remember any of them the following week. Just one played again and again, however, will drive everybody mental, so find a balance. Two or three is a good number to aim for, from scratch.

And find time for fun. If you're working hard on a complex, challenging new piece, make sure you leave a few minutes to run through something simple that you know well and enjoy playing. Don't hammer all the pleasure out of playing by over-rehearsing and killing it stone dead; strike a balance.

Also, don't forget the point – you're presumably rehearsing for something, even if it's a vague aim to one day play in public, or just to be able to get all the way through side two of *Ziggy Stardust* without stopping. Whatever your goal, make sure your rehearsal efforts are heading towards it, rather than just rehearsing for the sake of rehearsing. That's expensive, time-wasting and soul-destroyingly tedious to the point of making band members think very hard about finding another outfit who actually have a strategy.

Rehearsals are necessary, bordering on essential. But they shouldn't be a chore. Be smart, be considerate and be directed and you'll enjoy them a lot more. Even if you still have to tell the drummer to shut up a few times.

BAND MEETINGS

Meetings? For a band? What is this, the civil service? We're not a corporation, we're a musical, er, thingummy! Don't force me to act like The Man, maaaan!

Yes, it sounds a bit corporate and boring, but a band meeting can be some of the most productive time you can spend.

It doesn't involve instruments and making a noise, and is all the better for it. Ideally, a band meeting is the time where you consider your direction, set your goals, discuss your influences, suggest new material, review the line-up, talk through any musical conflicts, smooth over any personality clashes, and get the chance to have an adult conversation longer than three words with your bandmates.

So you're still trying to do all that between numbers in your regular rehearsals? No, no, no. A very bad idea indeed, for all the reasons stated in the rehearsals section. That's not what a rehearsal's for – that's what a band meeting's for.

The most convenient and convivial place to have these is often a pub. This is fine. Usually.

First, remember that you're supposed to be talking; trying to combine it with a gig by another band, a loud jukebox or Sky Sports on full blast is not going to work. Try to find a sleepy old boozer where you can hear each other (but preferably not one that reeks of disinfectant and is full of old blokes coughing and their smelly dogs – somewhere that you won't mind spending a couple of hours is handy).

Also, it's a conversation not a piss-up. The bass player may have a mighty thirst or the singer may be on an absinthe kick, but try to stay reasonably sober for at least as long as it takes to iron out the important points. Having a band meeting that nobody can remember and waking up the next morning with a black eye, a shocking headache, a left shoe full of chicken masala and the drummer's girlfriend/boyfriend is not the best way to achieve a long and friendly band relationship.

One thing you do need is an agenda. Yes, more businessy rubbish, but it doesn't have to be on headed paper with 'AOB' at the end – it just has to be a rough mental plan of what you need to chat about; all the issues that need sorting out while you've got a chance to consider them properly as a band. Try to get through the lot, then you'll feel that you've made some progress.

If the beer kicks in and things get random before you've discussed all the issues, it's a wasted opportunity.

Make your band meetings productive, and make them regular. Not twice a week, of course, but once every few months is good, and maybe more often if things are changing fast (songs, members, vast success, massive failure, decision to change direction and become an all-flute death metal outfit, that sort of thing).

Naturally, there are other types of band-related meetings. There are the ones where you're sussing out a potential member, pre-audition (see the previous Auditions section for more on that) and want to get an idea of whether they'd be a good fit personally before you judge their instrumental prowess. Again, keep them organised, have a list in your head or on a bit of paper of all the things you need to ask, and keep them fairly sober. You don't want to end the night telling a possible new member that they're your best friend in the world ever, then realising the following morning that there's no way your reggae act needs a xylophone player.

Then there's the other sort: the sacking meeting. Often tricky, this one. It's usually two meetings anyway; first, after a sort of rough consensus has been agreed, there should be a full band meeting, minus the offending member, to make sure everyone's in agreement that you need to drop the person in question.

Then it comes to the face-to-face 'You're fired' moment. First, who's going to do it? If there's a band-leader, it's up to them. If it's more egalitarian than that, you need to think hard. All of the band turning up can feel a bit like bullying. One or two might work; but depending on what band relationships are like, this can mean the ones who are most friendly to the sackee, and will therefore be kindest, or those who aren't and therefore won't give a stuff about delivering the bad news.

In any case, it'll be a sticky situation. Though not always; often when relationships have deteriorated to that point, it's a two-way thing. Then it's a race to see who can get in first. "You're sacked!" "No I'm not, I resign." It's by no mean unusual to get the response "Well, I was thinking about leaving anyway" in these circumstances, in which case an entirely civilised and amicable divorce can be arranged and everybody can get on with their lives.

If it's likely to come out of the blue, however, either because the victim is utterly insensitive and hasn't noticed that everyone else hates them, or because a sudden direction change has been decided from on high and they're no longer required, you need to make extra sure that drink is not involved – tempers can flare badly after a few – and that it's handled professionally and sensibly. Don't make it personal, no matter how irritating the person may be, and make sure you're absolutely clear. Mumbling something vague and running away will just cause confusion and you might have to end up sacking them again, just to sort it all out. Or, not realising they've been fired, they might turn up to the next gig or rehearsal to find somebody else occupying their spot. Deeply awkward.

Exactly the same thing applies if you're the one doing the resigning. Be straight, be professional and don't beat around the bush. No matter how tempting it is to have a tantrum – onstage mid-gig resignations are not unknown – you never know when you'll run across somebody again, whether it's as a support band, at a rehearsal studio, or just to borrow a bit of gear in a hurry. So make it civilised, and make it quick. Say your piece, wish them well, then get out. Don't linger for a valedictory pint or several, because that's when it'll all end in tears. Leave, and let them get on with muttering about how they always hated you anyway and were planning your replacement.

So can we call this meeting to order? Thank you.

CHAPTER 5

LIVE AND MILDLY DANGEROUS

Why play live? Because we're humans, that's why. Our species has evolved a uniquely strong sense of community; a social bond that makes us seek approval, praise and recognition from our peers by displaying our talents or abilities.

But let's be less po-faced and anthropological about it. Playing live is a bloody good laugh. For many of us, it's the whole point of being a musician; those moments when you're up on stage make all the dull stuff worthwhile. When the sweat and adrenalin are flowing, it can be the best thing ever.

Some don't agree; not all musicians enjoy the rough-and-tumble of live performance, and there's no rule that says you have to.

And it does have more than its fair share of dodgy bits, from the hassles of booking gigs to the sometimes teeth-achingly exasperating business of getting gear and musicians together in the same place at the same time, not to mention the technical faff of getting everything working properly, then trying to achieve a half-decent sound.

Hopefully by the end of this chapter you'll have picked up, or refreshed your memory about, a few ways of making a gig into an enjoyable event rather than a hellish mess of tangled cables, idiot promoters and absent bassists.

It's sometimes irritating and occasionally embarrassing, but that live gig is a fine target to aim for, particularly if you're in the sort of band that rehearses frequently but without any particular direction in mind.

And when you do start playing live regularly, you'll realise that the pressure and enforced discipline of trying to get through a set seamlessly, complete with simultaneous starts and stops, on-key harmonies and proper dynamics, will improve your playing more than any number of rehearsals. The very fact that when you're on stage you can't stop a song halfway through and go over a dodgy bit again (or at least you really, really shouldn't) will sharpen up your musical reflexes. If you're in a band you'll find that you start to listen to the other players, as they will to you, and anticipate or react to their subtler nuances.

That's what that hoary old phrase 'paying your dues', which wrinkly ex-pros trot out every so often, actually means – playing in front of an audience, again and again, until you're confident and skilled. That's what playing live does, and that's why everybody should give it a go.

If you're lucky enough to see a really good band at their peak, on a good night, you'll appreciate the alchemy that live playing can create. Everybody steps up to the challenge and pulls out a performance that's better than they themselves thought possible. Transcendental, dude. Wow.

Even if you're not in the Grateful Dead it's pretty, er,

groovy. So get on your best gigging outfit and get on stage. Here's how.

HOW TO GET GIGS

It's one of the basic questions. As soon as you get a few songs together and have rehearsed them until you're fairly confident you can get through without everything falling apart, the time comes to get out there and play live. Which involves that tricky puzzle – getting gigs.

It's not an insoluble problem. You just phone your manager, who gives your booking agency a call. They make a few enquiries to see if the local stadium, the Albert Hall or the O2 Arena are free, then it's all systems go.

You say you haven't got a manager? Or a booking agent? I bet you don't even own a helicopter. In that case, things are slightly more difficult. But not impossible; there are bands playing gigs all over the place all the time. Somebody must have found the solution.

In fact, it's easier than you think. But you do have to be organised, proactive and reasonably persistent. You also need to have a good idea about what sort of gigs you want to get, where and why. Oh great, yet more questions.

So let's start with the major one. Why do you want to get gigs? Is it to earn money, to get career-boosting exposure, or just to have fun?

If you answered 'all of the above', you might want to set your sights a little lower, at least to start with. But one out of three ain't bad, as Meat Loaf (nearly) sang.

If your aim is to earn money, you need to be

entertaining and crowd-pleasing. That often involves playing cover versions (see Chapter 4 for more on that. Are you reading backwards or something?).

You can sometimes make a little money by playing original material, but it's much tougher, particularly if you're not a bunch of skinny 19-year-olds with pointy cheekbones, happily living in a freezing squat on out-of-date Pot Noodles and an unrealistic hope of stardom. That sort of band will sometimes ride a wave of hype and play the sort of hipster venues where you get paid something. The rest of us might as well forget it.

But if you're playing a set comprised entirely or mostly of covers, whether they're party favourites, jazz standards, blues classics or rock anthems, there's a pretty decent gig circuit, particularly around bigger cities.

Your first step – and this applies to all gig-getting, really – is to check out the gig listings and see where the same sort of bands as you are playing. If you have the time and energy, go and visit them. It's usually fun and it'll give you a far better idea of what you're up against in terms of set lengths, musical competence and audience expectations.

For instance, if your ramshackle rockabilly outfit usually turns up to knock out a half-hour set in old jeans and scruffy jumpers, it's well worth knowing that the venue you'd like to play at expects well-groomed stage costumes, a slick stage act and three one-hour sets. Or vice versa. Your two-hour hair metal extravaganza, complete with lasers, spandex-clad go-go girls, dry ice and a revolving drum kit, simply may not fit in the local pub, who may well be more used to three old boys belting out Irish rebel songs round the piano in the corner.

It's also valuable having a word with that night's band if you're in a potential venue. They shouldn't see you as rivals, as they've almost certainly done the same thing themselves. Just offer to buy them a drink and ask what the venue's like to play, and you should glean all sorts of useful info about load-ins, soundchecks, money, dressing rooms (or not), the audience, how far ahead they book and, vitally, what the landlord or promoter likes.

You may come across the occasional moron who refuses to give you any information at all on the basis that you'll steal their income; remember them, as sooner or later you could well end up sharing a stage at a festival or multi-band gig. That's when they come crawling over to borrow a battery or a pair of pliers and you remind them of their previous unhelpfulness. 'Instant Karma' is not just a John Lennon song, you know.

So you've identified some venues, and you've done enough research to know who to contact. Now we run into the giant catch-22 of gigging: you can only get gigs if you're popular. But you can't get popular without gigging. How do you break out of that vicious circle?

That's where the second of our two categories comes in – gigging to gain exposure. Before you start to play the bigger and more lucrative places, you'll have to play some venues strictly for their audience-building potential, so when the promoter asks "How many people can you bring along?" you can truthfully answer with a plausible and economically viable number. Then, of course, you double it, as is entirely expected.

LIVE AND MILDLY DANGEROUS

This stage isn't quite as vital as it used to be; there are other ways of building a potential audience, like Facebook, Myspace and the like (there's more on that later on in this chapter). Of course, your first gig is always a bit of a leap into the unknown, so it does make a lot more sense to start with a few low-key, unpaid gigs to sharpen up your act and get your name around in local music circles.

Doing your first ever gig at a large, important, venue is impossibly brave; or more likely foolhardy. It's like jumping in the deep end. With sharks. And piranhas.

Even megastars have trouble – there's a famous line from the film *Woodstock* where Crosby, Stills, Nash & Young are tuning up for their set at the legendary festival. "This is only the second time we've played in front of people..." confessed Stephen Stills "...and we're scared shitless."

None of your first few gigs are likely to be at Woodstock, unless you've got a really good line in blarney and a Tardis, but the same thing applies. Get the nerves, cock-ups and poor live song choices out of the way without too much pressure, and start to build a buzz in a few little places before starting the push upwards.

Of course, your amazingly good demo will help get you gigs, won't it? Won't it? If you haven't got a decent-sounding recording you're on a hiding to nothing, so check out the chapter later on which deals with that bit and make sure you've got a respectable recording to your name. Put it online somewhere easily accessible, because the days of posting out crackly cassettes are long gone; promoters want a link to a demo they can listen to at their leisure, instantly and at decent quality. Technology. Marvellous, isn't it?

If you're intending to move from smaller venues to bigger, better or more highly paid ones, you'll need to plan out your strategy and allow a decent amount of time for it all to happen. A rule of thumb is that the bigger the venue, the further ahead they'll book. The bloke at the Old Midget & Spoonbill round the corner might have next Friday week free, but you're looking at many months for more professional places. It's not unknown for the better-attended venues to book big nights such as New Year's Eve a full year or more ahead, so keep an eye on that when you're planning your calendar.

If you're relatively new on the scene, you'll probably get booked for nights earlier in the week at first anyway; no decent promoter would put on an untried act in a prime slot.

Unless... here's an advantage you might have if you're seriously organised and mobile. What if a promoter at a venue you're booked at a few months hence calls up and says "Er, lads, tonight's act has just perished in a horrible dishwasher accident. Any chance you're free?"

This could be your big chance, or at least your medium-sized one. But can you do a last-minute gig? Are you well-rehearsed and tight? Is all your gear packed and ready to go at a moment's notice, or is it in a tangle under the bed? Can you get in touch with everybody instantly, or does the keyboard player's job as an alligator wrestler mean he can't be contacted at work? Does the singer always watch *Gardeners' World* on a Friday evening, so he doesn't fancy going out? Are you all mobile or is it a nightmare of waiting for buses and blagging lifts?

If you can get all that straightened out, make sure that promoters know you're available for short-notice gigs. Bands pull out of gigs surprisingly often and you'll stand a much better chance of getting booked in a decent slot if you've previously filled a last-minute gap. The promoter will feel that you've got them out of a hole and ought to repay the favour. If you've been any good, of course. Turning up at the last minute to replace the band for Aunt Mavis's 80th and blasting through your usual set of Sex Pistols, Damned and Clash covers may not be quite so effective in getting a rebooking. Funny, though.

But what if your thoughts on gigs are not quite as directed and ambitious – what if you just fancy doing the occasional live thing to show off in front of your mates/partners/relatives and get a bit of light exercise?

That's not quite as easy as it sounds. You still have to be organised enough to get along to a venue complete with all members and a sufficiency of functional equipment, and roughly on time would be good too.

You still need some sort of demo – though recording can be enjoyable too – and almost certainly a web presence. And have an idea of where to play and what it's likely to require.

All of which is just the sort of prep that you want for any kind of hobby or activity. Do you turn up to play golf late and without clubs? Do you fettle your classic car with an old knife and fork, plus a rusty pickaxe for the big jobs? No. You do a bit of pre-activity sorting out, so when you do the thing you enjoy, it's easy and hassle-free.

So take it a bit seriously. Look like you mean it. Even if you don't really. Promoters and landlords are understandably less keen to indulge bands who aren't that bothered about whether they bring a full house or not.

If you're only in it for the amusement, you do, however, have the option of taking gigs that other bands or artists may not bother with; the London music scene, particularly, is full of venues or promoters who pack in five or so bands in an evening on a contract that ensures that none of them will ever make any money unless they bring 4,000 fans. The promoter and the venue will profit, but the bands won't. Cue much moaning about evil music business scum.

However, it's not a secret and unless you're especially stupid nobody sees this sort of gig as a stepping-stone to anything except a small overdraft. If you just fancy getting out of an evening and doing a bit of playing to sharpen up, loosen up or test out a new member these gigs are fine.

So you share the bill with a punk-reggae outfit, some blisteringly loud grunge wannabes, three girls with a beatbox and a Swedish teenage punk band. So what? It's better than sitting on the sofa and watching yet another dull detective series on telly. You could also make a few contacts, see some reasonable bands and have a couple of beers with your mates. This is not a terrible thing.

You could also consider playing venues that don't usually have bands on: village, church or school halls, youth clubs or social clubs, even a local farmer's barn if the weather's half decent. Once you're not tied to making money or raising your profile the world's your lobster. Got a mate who's having an outdoor summer party? Excellent. Warn their neighbours and scrounge a generator.

You can promote your own events too. Just hire a hall or a pub's function room and ask a couple of other bands to share the bill. Maybe make it a regular event. Why not? You could even start charging a bit on the door to cover costs. You're unlikely to make a lot of money, if any, but it'll be a good evening and if you get organised with things like a PA and a few lights if necessary, it shouldn't be too much hassle.

But whether you're driven by money, ambition or fun, remember one thing: it's supposed to be enjoyable. If by the time you get on stage you're frazzled, knackered and grumpy then the audience will pick up on that and you'll all have a horrible time. Get your organisation done early, and make sure everything on the night is present, correct and working. Then have a great time.

That includes booking gigs. Make sure you know what the deal is with money, timings, gear, other bands and so on well in advance. Get it in writing if at all possible. That'll make it all much simpler.

And if you have a good time and get a decent crowd, don't forget to ask for a rebooking as soon as possible; on the night if you can, while the landlord or promoter is still in a good mood.

At its worst, booking gigs can be a nasty combination of apathy and bureaucracy, but once you get going you'll find it much easier. You'll build up a few contacts and, who knows, they may even call and offer you a gig occasionally once you've been around a while. Be flexible, be sorted, and of course once you're on stage be exciting and entertaining. Or, if all else fails, learn some decent jokes...

GOING SOLO

In some ways getting gigs as a singleton is easier, if often more nerve-wracking and work-intensive, than as a band.

Obviously, there's only one of you to do everything – unless, of course, you can bribe, wheedle or threaten a partner, mate or fan to take some of the workload, which is not a bad trick if it doesn't cause too much collateral damage to your personal life. If you're the sort of person who's liable to throw a tantrum or a massive sulk when everything doesn't go 100% to plan, maybe it's better to tackle the administrative stuff yourself before you drive everybody round you to distraction. Or physical violence. It wouldn't be the first time.

But getting a little highly strung is possibly excusable, because it's just your reputation on the line if it all goes wrong. No hiding behind the bass player for you.

All of the gig-getting advice in the previous section applies to you too (you haven't read it? Get back there right now. There'll be a test later). But you do actually have a few advantages over the band-bound. First, there can be a more gradual progression towards a full headline set as a solo act than as a group. You can start off with a couple of songs at an open mic night or a folk, blues or jazz club, then advance gradually to a short support set, then finally, if you get that far, are any good and can be bothered, you're likely to get offered a full headline set and maybe, possibly, some money. Which, of course, you don't have to split four or five ways. Result.

You also have a much wider selection of potential venues in which to find gigs. While a full band tends to take up a lot of space and make a large amount of noise, you can squeeze into a corner and play at a pleasantly conversational volume. Of course, that doesn't mean that you can't amplify yourself to fill a bigger venue, or even drag in a few other musicians from time to time to increase your musical range and power.

But on your own, your gig hit list can include restaurants, wine bars, intimate parties, tiny pubs and clubs, and anywhere else that people gather, outdoors or in, where a bit of music's likely to be appreciated.

Of course, this is easier if you're a solo artist who plays something relatively portable. Your church organ speciality may not work so well round a camp fire.

So, as mentioned previously, your first line of attack ought probably to be places that already book your type of act. They'll know the drill, the audience will be receptive, and you'll feel reasonably at home. Lovely.

Practically, again as mentioned before, you'll need a well-recorded demo, a web presence of a relatively professional standard, and enough material to pull off a set of the length required, whether that's a 20-minute support slot or an all-night entertainment extravaganza.

One thing that's useful for a solo artist is a few recommendations from others. This doesn't happen so much with bands; they tend to act as their own little cliques, shuffling around glaring at each other like opposing gangs in the school playground. But solo artists are much more gregarious and the camaraderie tends to be greater; maybe it's the fact that the mere fact of turning up unaccompanied is appreciated as being an act of creative bravery. Or maybe it's that they're desperate for someone to talk to.

Whichever it is, you'll find that if your set goes down well, your fellow artists may well offer a few kind words, and may even be willing, once you've played the same places a few times and got to know each other a bit, to put in a good word with a promoter. Strictly on a reciprocal basis, of course; they'll expect you to do the same thing for them. So beware of being too gushing about somebody that you think is actually rubbish in exchange for a good reference; it may come back to bite you when you tell a favourite venue that they're superb and they empty the place within the first two numbers. They won't be booked back again, but neither will you.

If promoters hear good things about you from an artist they know is trustworthy, however, it can open a lot of doors. And all those short sets at singers' nights and so on are a good way of building a reputation and making useful contacts. As a solo artist you can turn up, tune up and be ready to play in the time it takes the average band to park their car and find the drummer's hi-hat stand, let alone start loading their gear in. Make the most of that flexibility and speed.

Although don't develop too much of a hit-and-run style at open mic nights – it's deeply frowned upon to arrive, play your songs and leave immediately. Not staying to hear anybody else is considered the height of selfish bad manners, so be considerate.

Your cost base is much lower, too. If you need to make money from your gigs, the sure-fire way to do it is to go solo. No sharing the fee, no gear to hire or vans to park, and no roadies to pay.

An example: in the late '70s eccentric, brilliant electric guitarist Robert Fripp left prog-rock dinosaur King Crimson, with its articulated lorries full of equipment, huge light shows and massive entourage, and returned with what he called 'a small, mobile, intelligent unit'. Back in the late '70s you couldn't do half the looping and multi-tracking that's possible today, but even then he managed to do several well-received solo tours armed with a smallish box full of tape recorders and electronics. He often played unusual venues such as pizza parlours and barber's shops, and for more local venues would turn up on the train with his box of tricks and his guitar. He managed to confuse audiences expecting pompous rock nicely, but importantly he also managed to earn a reasonable living from his remarkably minimal set-up.

And talking of unusual venues, that's your other advantage. Is there a local restaurant or wine bar that would be improved by a bit of live music? Would your local pub have a small back room or corner of a bar that would make a good impromptu venue? It never hurts to ask. If you've got a few musician friends, so much the better. Start a small regular session and you'll begin to grow an audience, and quite possibly a small queue of keen potential performers.

Amplification is a tricky thing here. None at all is easy, and keeps things pure and simple. But the world's a surprisingly noisy place when it's just your voice and an instrument. A restaurant's espresso machine can drown you out *al presto*; even the clinking of knives and forks and the hum of conversation gets pretty loud. And pubs, with their noisy glass-clinking patrons and loud beer-induced jollity, are another step further up the decibel scale.

Sadly, the sound system in most places that aren't usual music venues will be of little help; it's designed to diffuse background music across the widest possible area, rather than allow your vocals to be heard immediately in front of you. And even plugging in a microphone can be tricky. So you can end up carting a PA from place to place, which slightly defeats the object of being mobile and flexible. The golden rule ought to be to use the bare minimum possible.

Luckily, some of the latest amplification systems are amazingly light, powerful and portable. Many designed specifically for solo artists have inputs for a microphone and an instrument, usually guitar, a decent selection of effects, some sort of anti-feedback system and even an extendable stand to get them up above the audience's heads – and more importantly, often come with wheels and a trolley handle so you can cart them around without crippling yourself or having to hire a beefy mate with a van.

Of course if you're playing somewhere regularly, it ought to be possible to leave a speaker, amp and bag of leads in a back room or cellar so you can just drag it out and plug it in every time. Don't leave anything portable and obviously valuable, though; microphones tend to walk, effects pedals wander, and a guitar-shaped case is a theft waiting to happen.

But never mind the unpleasant side of human nature; focus on the enjoyment of making a perfect connection between your music and an audience. And enjoy your gigs, whether they're in a tiny bar or on a festival stage, in the smug feeling that you won't have to share a small van with a sweaty drummer on the way home.

MATURE MUSO TRICKS

Let's face it, none of us are getting any younger. And if you're reading this book, chances are that you're already at a reasonable stage of maturity.

This is not a problem; there may be a little more bulk here and there, there may be a little less hair, but you've gained wisdom, taste, an appreciation of the finer things in life and an ability to get on with life without giving much of a stuff about what anybody else thinks.

However, when tackling the gig circuit, and sometimes other musical areas, one occasionally happens across the attitude that anybody past 25 is a hopeless old fool with zero credibility and the talent of a woodlouse. And sometimes these people are in charge of booking gigs, doing the sound or some other quite necessary role, so you need to cope with them.

Luckily, age will have given you the patience to deal with such callow youths without administering the firm clip round their ear they undoubtedly need. And also, luckily, you'll no doubt have mastered the combination of deviousness, wit and guile to get them to do whatever you need without physical violence of any kind.

The first technique to master, however, is avoiding the issue entirely. Like Obi-Wan Kenobi in *Star Wars*, there are certain mind tricks you can employ to make yourself seem exactly the sort of band that they're looking for, rather than a bunch of useless old duffers.

For a start, why are you talking to this particular fluffy-faced youth? Is it because you're trying to get them to book you in for a gig at a venue they run? Think hard. If the booking agent is a 19-year-old, there's a strong chance that the audience will be as well. Do you really want to strut your stuff in front of an unreceptive bunch of teenies?

If the answer is 'yes', or the scenario is that somehow a perfectly grown-up venue has employed somebody who thinks that any band before 2008 is ancient history, then you need to make yourselves look young and cool. Or at least old and interesting. Legendary, in fact.

Seasick Steve, the grizzle-bearded bluesman, is a superb example of this tactic. Taking advantage of youngsters' relative lack of knowledge of history, he arrived fully formed as an Authentic Blues Legend, complete with dungarees and tractor-branded hat. The fact that Steven Wold, as he was christened, spent the 1980s and 1990s as a session musician and recording engineer with indie bands like Modest Mouse was quietly glossed over, along with spells in Paris and Norway and other inconveniently non-blues-legend type facts; as far as the younger generation was concerned he might as well have been a contemporary of Robert Johnson, still living in a delta shack and picking a bale or two of cotton just before strolling on stage at Glastonbury to play a set.

This isn't knocking Seasick Steve; on the contrary, he's an extremely fine musician and a very clever bloke. But it's a great example of what public relations dweebs call 'reputation management'. In other words, if you want to be treated as a legend, start acting like one.

Got a link (however tenuous) with somebody famous? Big it up. And don't be shy about quietly glossing over boring or off-message stuff. If you once shared a studio with an ex-member of a huge band, say so. Don't mention that you were actually in there mending the plumbing or selling them a new sign for their car park. Nobody needs to know that bit.

Remember, this is the entertainment business. Everything's provisional and truth is strictly optional. As the famous quote goes: 'The secret of success is sincerity. Once you can fake that, you've got it made.' So when it comes to your band CV, be adventurous and be entertaining. Being utterly truthful is a long way down the list.

So as far as the youngsters go you're an amazing, groundbreaking, legendary band or artist that they've never heard of because they're too young. That's settled then. It may not be strictly 100% accurate, but it's an awful lot better than "We're three chartered accountants and an electrician doing this for a hobby."

When you've got your gig, of course, you may well come across other junior life forms. Sound engineers, for instance. It does often seem that the younger they are, the more likely they are to wind the volume up to the point that your audience has to escape to the next-door bar before their eardrums shatter or their bowels let go thanks to the trouser-flapping bass.

This is not a good thing, for several reasons – firstly, it's boring to play to an empty room; secondly, the volume's likely to be punishing on stage too, which will leave you with at least a day of ringing ears, earplugs or not; and thirdly, it'll flatten out any subtleties you may be attempting and make your painstakingly rehearsed musical interplay sound like someone hammering nails into a pig. Even if you can actually hear each other, which is pushing your luck a bit with the average pub monitor system.

This needs nipping in the bud. When you notice it at sound check time, don't mutter grumpily and do nothing; be clear and definite about the fact that it's too loud. Delegate one member to make a reasoned but very firm case for keeping the volume to manageable levels. If necessary, talk to the landlord or promoter and explain that you're bringing people along who will not stay to buy drinks if the volume is excessive.

You may get a reputation for being difficult. This is not necessarily a bad thing, provided you're able to back that up with also being good. Cantankerous and crap is a poor combination, however. Be polite, be generous (maybe you could compliment the engineer on how good his monitor mix/use of reverb/haircut is) but don't take any nonsense.

Of course, young people do have their uses: carrying stuff; spending ten minutes doing a website, MySpace page or Facebook presence, which would take you three days; and of course coming along to your gigs, being impressed by your vast knowledge and ancient wisdom, and telling all their mates how good you are. Those are all rather fine.

GEAR AND ENGINEERS

So you've got your first gig. You've rehearsed in your usual studio/shed/hall for months. You turn up, load in your regular gear, wire it up as normal, and immediately sound appallingly, unlistenably bad. Like a gang of weasels fighting in a metal dustbin. Utterly different from your established, carefully honed sound. What, as Marvin Gaye might have put it, is going on?

You've just found out the first rule of playing live – your sound will be hugely variable, and not usually in a good way. Part of that is, of course, down to the person twiddling the knobs on the mixing desk out front. More on that in a minute. But a large chunk of that is down to you, your gear and your experience.

The first clue is the word 'usual'. You always rehearse in the same place, you probably set up in the same way week in week out, and you're used to getting a reliably decent sound there. But that, of course, doesn't mean you'll get a decent sound anywhere else. Before you play live for the first time, it's well worth trying a different rehearsal venue to see how you cope with unfamiliar circumstances. And try setting up as though at a live gig – amps all facing forward, drums at the back, singer out front. You know the drill. It's funny how different that makes you sound. Most bands rehearse facing towards each other in a circle; this is marvellous to hear the finer points of each other's playing but distinctly flattering when compared to a gig, where the amps will be at opposite sides of the stage, the volume level may vary wildly and there'll almost certainly be monitors sending back random bits of your sound to add to the confusion.

So try to simulate a gig. Set up as though live, start playing, then, if possible, go out front to where the audience would be and have a listen (make sure you've got a long enough lead if you're a guitarist or bassist. While bringing a pile of amps crashing down on the drummer's head may be uproariously funny, you don't want to damage your amp just before a gig. Or your drummer). If you do play drums or keyboards, see if somebody else can fill in for you for a moment so you can have a listen.

You may be surprised by the sound of the whole band. You'll almost certainly think your own part is too quiet. It isn't. If this sound-sorting exercise just ends up as a war of eardrum attrition in which everybody sneakily turns up their amps until it's painfully loud, you've missed the point. You're used to hearing your own part louder than everybody else's because you're right next to your amp, drum kit or monitor speaker. Hearing the whole thing as one piece is different. And it should be. While you're all set up gig-style, this would be a good time to do a quick bit of recording. Put a recorder or a pair of microphones in the centre (there's more on how to do this in a chapter or so) and record a few numbers. Then listen back, and have a chat about levels. Twiddle, record, repeat.

Of course the baseline volume you'll probably be used to working towards is your drummer, if you have one. Drums are a loud instrument, and although drummers do vary in volume from subtle jazz brush-swishers to hard rock pounders with sticks like tree trunks, they all still make a fair amount of racket. Bass, keyboard and guitar amps will have to be loud enough to compete; PA systems need to be powerful enough to get the singer heard over it all.

This is at a rehearsal, of course. But at many gig venues this is not actually the case. When the drums and all the amps are miked up and keyboards and bass are plugged directly into the mixing desk, there's no real necessity for amps to be at drummer-beating volume. Oddly, you might find yourself playing more quietly live than at a rehearsal. Make sure you know how to cope when this is the case; if you're one of those guitarists who relies on their amp being set at a certain volume to get the right tone, you'll have to experiment to see if you can get close to that tone when required to play at a quieter or even louder level. It's really best do this on your own – turn up to a rehearsal a bit early or book an hour's solo practice, otherwise your endless knob-twiddling and experimental widdly-widdly riffage will drive everybody else in the band absolutely mental. Do try to play real riffs and chords when getting your sound right, though, so you can compare like with like.

Being quiet on stage is a very good thing; it means that everything's more controllable. When there's a great deal of volume coming off the stage the engineer's options will be limited. When most of the sound is going through the mixing desk, however, they'll be able to tweak what the audience hears to make you sound at your best.

So try turning down. Playing quietly is a very useful exercise; you'll start hearing subtleties in your own music that you never knew were there, and you'll be able to hear each other far better too. Dynamics will start to become more achievable and once the excitement is no longer artificially boosted by massive volume, you'll start to find better ways of making your set entertaining.

Many well-known bands play surprisingly quietly on stage nowadays; the days when the likes of The Who and Led Zeppelin had walls of amps blasting away behind them are long gone. That was only a short-lived phase anyway, necessitated by the fact that the PAs at early stadium rock gigs couldn't cope with the bass or guitar signals very well, so the onstage amps had to be loud enough to reach the back rows unassisted. This is why almost all survivors of that dinosaur rock era are almost totally stone deaf. As the joke goes, Pete Townshend's hearing is so bad that The Who may have to be rechristened The What?

Pop veterans Blondie, who are still busily gigging all over the world, are a good example of this way of working; these days they all wear discreet in-ear monitors on stage, their famously loud hooligan of a drummer Clem Burke is tucked away behind sound-deflecting Perspex panels and the guitarists play through tiny, low-wattage amps miked through the PA. From the audience's perspective it's as loud as any other band, but on stage you could have a nice mid-song natter with Debbie Harry without raising your voice.

Another side-effect of lower volume is less gear.

LIVE AND MILDLY DANGEROUS

Bands have a tendency to indulge in a nuclear arms race with equipment: the guitarist gets a loud amp, so the drummer adds another bass drum; the bassist gets a second cabinet, so the guitarist upgrades to a stack; the drummer starts using thicker sticks so the keyboard player upgrades his amp by a couple of hundred watts... and so on, until you're playing at roof-shaking volume and everyone's wearing industrial ear defenders. Just stop it. Stop it right now.

There are loads of very good guitar amps around now that sound just great at tiny volume. Bassists also have the option of light, portable good-sounding amps. Drummers could move over to one of the highly portable and surprisingly decent-feeling electronic kits that are available. Or just get a smaller, more compact kit and go easy on the caveman routine.

Whether you go down the whole low-volume route or just turn down a couple of notches, you'll play better. And you'll have less gear to carry, set up and plug in. This means less time wasted messing around with stands, leads and mains extensions and more time rehearsing or soundchecking.

It's worth slimming down your set-up to play live anyway. It's easy to take tons of kit to a rehearsal, but do you really need those effects pedals that you rarely use, those broken leads you haven't quite got round to mending, and any of the rest of the contents of the big bag of random kit you cart about? Before you go gigging, fine-tune your gear and trim it down to the bare essentials. Yes, spare leads are useful, and other emergency equipment such as batteries, strings, picks, sticks and so on are vital, but keep it sensible. You should ideally put together a dedicated gig bag with all the supplies you need in it, tidily packed and ready for immediate use.

And practise setting up swiftly and efficiently. The quicker you can assemble your gear, the happier the sound engineer will be and the more time you'll get for a proper soundcheck.

Ah yes, the soundcheck. They're horrible. And boring. They often happen hours before your set, so it forces you all to turn up stupidly early and hang around for ages. They usually consist of a lot of 'one-two' into mikes and tedious hours of the drummer banging random bits of kit.

But they're a very necessary evil. If you want to sound any good, you have to let the engineer get some settings down and make sure everything's working properly. The time you want to sound your best is right at the beginning of your set when you're trying to grab everybody's attention, and you simply won't be able to do that without a soundcheck.

It's a time to be disciplined and professional too. Get set up and test that everything's working. If there's a problem with your gear, fix it swiftly and don't faff. Then shut up until you're asked to play something. A soundcheck is not a rehearsal, a chance to play all your favourite riffs, or a good time to mess about with your settings or twiddle with your effects.

One temptation to avoid after soundchecks is immediately hitting the bar. You've loaded in and set up, it's all ready to go, but you've probably got a couple of hours spare before your set, so it's all too tempting to say, 'Anybody fancy a pint then?' By your stage time you'll be distinctly wobbly; a sloppy set will ensue, and nobody will be terribly impressed. It is, however, a good time to find something to eat. Get a meal in well before you have to play so you've got time to digest it and you won't feel too sluggish on stage.

But let's take a closer look at the person taking charge of the soundcheck – the sound engineer. Usually supplied by the venue when you're playing smallish places, these folk vary wildly from helpful, clued-up professionals to brain-dead, tone-deaf lunatics with awful taste in music, questionable personal hygiene and clothing that's been rejected by a goth charity shop. You can probably guess which sort are more common.

But even at their worst they can be useful; they know where the plug sockets are, and which ones work and which don't; they should be able to at least get you sounding acceptable out front and let you hear yourselves on stage, even if you need to cajole them into hearing enough vocals, turning down the volume or not using so much echo that you sound like you're playing in a tin bath.

Be polite to them, even if they're hassled and grumpy; they are in charge of your sound. They are the people who can make you sound good, or they can simply not bother.

If you're lucky and/or organised you may have your own sound engineer. Make sure that this is discussed beforehand, ideally when the gig is booked. Engineers get rather protective of their own set-up; letting a stranger do the sound on your desk is a bit like handing over the keys to your prized car to someone you've just met in the pub. So if the venue's own man is present, your engineer will have to introduce themselves and do a bit of being friendly and knowledgeable and earn the respect of the in-house person a little before they take over their role.

And if you do have an engineer, make absolutely sure they turn up. If you're the only outfit playing that night, the in-house person may have taken the night off. They will not be happy about being dragged away from their rare evening out by a bunch of disorganised idiots. If they arrive at all, they'll be grumpy and your sound will be rubbish. Beware.

The secret of good gigging is to be prepared, organised and, above all, flexible. Stuff happens. Things break. Vital bits get lost. People can be late due to no fault of their own. Brain fade can hit even the most intelligent and sorted people. Don't let any of this faze you; overcome any problems as quickly and efficiently as possible and never, ever, lose your temper. It's supposed to be enjoyable. If you throw a strop, you'll play poorly and come across badly; not only will you have a horrible time, so will your audience. Stay calm, cool and collected. If you do need to have a serious word with someone in the band who's being a berk, save it for the next rehearsal and do it in a more considered manner. Onstage fights are highly amusing but don't do much for a band's longevity.

And remember to have a good time. Get the boring chores out of the way early, forget about the fact that you'll have to take all the gear down and pack it up straight after your set, and enjoy your moment in the spotlight. It's worth all the hassle. It really is.

GETTING FANS ALONG

You know exactly who's going to come to your gigs, of course. There's your long-suffering partner, and the familiar faces of the other band-members' significant others. A sibling or two, possibly. A few loyal mates. That bloke from work who feels duty bound to turn up after he confessed to liking live music.

Is that enough yet? Well, unless you're playing in a phone box, then no, it isn't. So how do you get more people to come and see you?

There's one very significant milestone in every band's early career – it's when they first spot a person in the audience who nobody in the band recognises. A total stranger! Somebody who paid their own money to come along and see a band without even being married to one of them! Brilliant!

That's the big hurdle, particularly if you're playing your own music. Doing covers of popular songs, or an entire tribute act, is an easier way to attract an audience, but it's a bit like riding on the shoulders of your heroes' reputations – people aren't coming to see you, really, but coming to hear the songs they love, played live. There's nothing wrong with that, and many a packed pub on a Friday night bears witness to how much fun that can be.

But if you write your own material (or just have more obscure taste in cover versions than the big pop hits) you've got to work a wee bit harder to get a crowd along.

The first method is, undoubtedly, just gigging. Gig often, support all manner of other bands, get bands with decent crowds of their own to support you, and you'll gradually build a reputation and a following. If you're any good, of course. You are world-shakingly brilliant, though, aren't you? Well-rehearsed, superb on stage, fantastic songs, nice trousers. Thought so. Just checking.

That's the old-fashioned way of doing it and although it can be a bit of a slog, it's tried and tested. But there are many more options these days. And there's no reason you can't combine any or all of them, depending on how much time you've got available.

Another way of getting your name around, and one you should certainly be exploring if you're gigging, is traditional marketing. Posters, flyers and listings in local papers and websites are all decent ways of getting your name out there. And you'll want more than just your name, naturally. Don't forget the basic facts: when you're playing (date and doors-open time), where you're playing (remember the post code for the sat-nav crowd), what sort of music you do (make sure it says 'live blues' or 'trad jazz' or whatever in big letters) and how much it costs to get in (people hate being surprised by expensive tickets, but if it's free make sure that's very prominent indeed).

If you're doing a poster, make it clear, attractive and readable from a good distance away. A3 is a good size if possible. Keep the colours to a few bold shades and the type large and legible, and try not to get too arty or enigmatic. It's not an expression of your inner Picasso, it's an information notice.

Flyers are a good thing. If you're really organised, try to print up a load of flyers for your next gig and distribute them at your current one. Small is fine – A5 or postcard size is plenty; you want people to pocket them. Put a few on each table; put a small pile by the door and on the bar. Again, keep it to basic information on your upcoming date(s), and make sure there's a link to your website, Facebook page, Myspace site or whatever if people want more information.

Ah yes, your website. You do have one, don't you? If not, get a move on. There are hundreds of easy ways to put together a basic but decent-looking website these days; you no longer have to hire a speccy nerd who talks in HTML code. Blogging platforms like Blogger, Tumblr, Wordpress and so on are pretty much a fill-in-the-blanks exercise. Facebook is often the first point of call for musicians, and you might find you don't need anything else. Soundcloud is a good place to store recordings, if you want to let people hear some of your stuff. Myspace used to be an enormously popular social site; it's less so now but has worked hard to keep its usefulness for bands, and offers a pretty solid and easy-to-use package.

Just take a look at what other musicians of a similar level to yourselves, or a level you'd like to be at, are doing. What does their web presence look like? Is it easy to navigate, clear and informative? Does it show off a little bit of their character and make you want to go to their gigs, buy their recordings and join their gang? It does? Copy that then.

Whatever you do, though, keep it concise. One advantage of the internet is that you can fill it with as much content as you like; unlike a sheet of paper, it's almost infinite. This is also a terrible temptation – it's all too easy to dribble on and on, boring everybody except yourself and producing lengthy, dense screeds of unreadable nonsense.

Keep thinking 'What's the aim?' and 'What am I trying to say here?' and then get your point(s) across in as straightforward a way as you can. What do you want people to do? Make sure you have what advertising people describe as a 'call to action' – in other words, leave your audience with a clear idea of what to do next. Want to get them to your gigs? Say so. Wish to sell them a music download or a CD? Make that clear. Don't waffle around the point: be obvious.

Which doesn't mean 'be dull' – a bit of wit and fun is a good thing (unless you're a Joy Division tribute act, of course). Keep it light, short and entertaining. There's no reason you can't add in a few bits of extra info or take the chance to give people some background on your influences, previous collaborations or ambitions. Just don't forget what the main focus is. A short list of what you're listening to at the moment, or some great albums by your biggest influences, would be very cool. Turning your website into a sort of sprawling free-form musical encyclopaedia wouldn't be. Like your live act, leave them wanting more.

Links are a good thing too. Venues pretty much all have their own websites – link to them. Link to other bands you may be sharing a bill with, link to people you admire or helpful local businesses like your neighbourhood music shop or rehearsal studio. And ask for links in return. All of this will help push your website up the search rankings so it's easier for fans to find you.

And once they've found you, keep them coming back. Use emails to ping regular updates to potential gig-goers; harvest addresses mercilessly and build a mailing list. Again, keep your emails short and entertaining, and make sure all the basic facts are on there. And double-check it before you hit 'send'. Spelling errors, formatting cock-ups, non-functional links and omitting vital bits of info will quickly get all your emails moved straight into the spam bin. Watch out for the size of your messages too. Attaching a huge photo file, logo or whatever will irritate people who use a work email with a size limit, and may also get lost or flagged up as spam and automatically deleted.

A last-minute reminder email just before a gig is often useful; you should initially give people plenty of notice, but don't assume they'll remember to put it on their calendars. Give them another nudge two or three days beforehand.

Some rate Twitter highly as a way to get quick messages to a crowd; your mileage may vary, and it can be a hassle keeping it updated, but it's certainly something to consider if you think you can get enough people following you to make it worthwhile. Again, look at what your peers are doing. If they're finding it useful, what sort of stuff are they posting? It might work for you too.

In short, try everything. Bombard your potential fanbase with any and every form of promotional material you can think of. Put posters up, sprinkle flyers about, pester your local paper and all the music listings websites. Offer them incentives like music downloads, cheap CDs or other merchandise if they turn up to a gig. Start a loyalty card scheme where if they come to see you three times they get a half-price ticket. Try everything. Something, or some combination of things, will work. And that's how you get to that magic moment when somebody turns up to see you who's not a friend or relative. Now all you have to do is impress them enough to make them do it again.

CHAPTER 6

BETWEEN THE BUTTONS

Gear is important. Unless you're an unamplified singer you need some sort of apparatus to enable you to make music. And how good that apparatus is, whether a sousaphone or a synthesiser, makes a huge difference to how effective your music is. It's that simple. Usually.

Of course, there are exceptions. Everybody knows at least one irritating git who can make a cheap, badly beaten-up piece of rubbish sound better than the next player's £5,000 vintage masterpiece. And some of the best pieces of music ever have been recorded on some surprisingly dreadful equipment.

There's even a slightly sneery attitude towards knowing about your equipment in some circles, as though it's not part of being a 'proper' musician. This is, frankly, rubbish.

The right instrument – and here I'm including amplifiers, effects and other bits of electrickery – will make you sound better, play better and often be more confident in your ability and your image.

So no matter how nimble-fingered and well-practised you are, no matter how great your grip on musical theory and how enormous your charisma, you need something decent to strum, thump, plonk, blow into or otherwise make a racket with.

Even if your chosen kit is just to make an acoustic noise louder, it needs to make it louder in the right way. A gruff-voiced Jim Morrison-style singer will not want the same sort of amplification as a Joni Mitchellesque high-voiced soprano. And if your chosen acoustic métier is beatboxing, making noises with the backs of your knees or musical belching, the same applies. Although if it's the latter, please can we not share a microphone? Thanks.

There are also some people in this wide musical world of ours who have what some see as a slightly shameful secret regarding musical equipment. The fact is, they really like it. Really, really like it. In truth, they like it far more than the actual music. They're sometimes derided as gear obsessives, kit geeks and even plectrum-sniffers.

But hang on – this isn't a bad thing. Look at car enthusiasts, for instance. Some buy cars for their fabulous design but never look under the bonnet. Some buy them to drive fast, on a racetrack or a rally circuit, or slowly down pleasant country roads on a Sunday morning. Some buy them just to own them, often amassing a sizeable collection of one make or model. And some buy them as a pile of rusty bits and spend a very satisfying and lengthy period in the workshop fettling and finessing lumps of metal until they all fit together in the shape of a running, driving car. Generally, they then lose interest, sell the finished item and start looking around for another scrapyard survivor to resuscitate.

Are any of those enthusiasts worse than the others? Of course not. They're all having fun in their various ways. And the musical gear collector, restorer or historian is getting just as much satisfaction out of their pastime as anybody who plays endless highly enjoyable gigs with an instrument that's, er, brown and made by, um... no, can't remember.

Serious, respected professional musicians are no stranger to gear obsession either. Almost all have favourite instruments, but certainly some don't care much about the intricacies of technology or the idea of amassing a collection of classics, provided their trusty tool is on hand and in playable condition.

But others delve very deeply into the subject, building up huge museums of valuable or interesting instruments, endlessly trying out technical innovations or searching for the perfect tone, one tweak at a time.

There are plenty of eminent gearheads like Jeff Tweedy of Wilco, whose Chicago loft studio is famously rammed with obscure effects units, guitars and other quirky noisemakers; Neil Young, whose search for the ultimate tone has led to a hangar-sized warehouse absolutely full of little old Fender amplifiers; and multi-instrumental legend Ry Cooder, whose collection is legendary both for its size and for its range, covering every type of ethnic multi-stringed instrument imaginable and meandering into American roots instruments, custom-made specials and home-made one-off hybrids built from junk shop parts. In his storage facility there's a whole shelf just labelled 'weird stuff'. There's a great line from blues guitar queen Bonnie Raitt about him. Asked about her own guitar collection, she said "I'm not Ry Cooder, but I don't buy 'em for the colour either..."

Talking of which, I have it on good authority that somewhere in North London is a house owned by a highly paid technical specialist who tours with some of the world's biggest bands. Every room is crammed with guitars, which he buys on his days off between giant stadium gigs. And apparently he's aiming to collect a Stratocaster in every colour ever made, of every year, in every configuration of neck, electrics and hardware. And he's currently most of the way there. Now that's true devotion. And I hope his home contents insurance is up to date.

It's not just guitarists, mind. Rolling Stones drummer Charlie Watts, for instance, collects drum kits played by the legends of jazz – a hobby that needs both an in-depth knowledge of jazz percussionists and a great deal of room.

But while awe-inspiring, that might be a little extreme for most players. We really only need something simple, reliable and decent-sounding to start off with, then as our skill level increases, our tastes mature and our needs become more defined, we'll almost certainly want to move on to a more professional range of instrument. And maybe once we feel we're at a decent level, or because we want to treat ourselves, we might just stretch to something vintage or hand-made.

So here are a few ideas that might help you choose, buy, use, maintain and eventually dispose of your gear. Not always painlessly – I still regret selling several well-loved items while skint or bored, and buying quite a few others in outbreaks of spur-of-the-moment idiocy – but at least you'll be armed with a little background knowledge.

BETWEEN THE BUTTONS

Remember, you're only as good as what people hear; and what they're hearing is you, via your instrument. That's certainly worth thinking quite hard about.

NEW GEAR

So you want to buy a bit of new kit. It's simple. You go to a shop, you hand over some money, they give you what you want, you go home. Everybody's happy.

Except it's not really that simple, as we all know. What if they haven't got the exact thing you want? What if something goes wrong with it? What if they've got it, but someone else is offering it cheaper? And there are many, many more possibilities that can make buying new stuff into a large shopping bag of trouble.

However, let's try to untangle the process a little by looking at the various places you can buy your necessaries, starting with your local music shop.

If you've got a good one of these, treasure it. A decent music shop can be a tremendous source of information, advice, spares, contacts, band-forming potential, repairs and general bonhomie.

Ideally, this shop will be clean, bright and spacious, its owner friendly and flexible on prices, his staff knowledgeable yet never patronising, and his stock well kept and wide-ranging. There will be a noticeboard covered in useful contacts for musicians, bands and gigs, and there will also be a repair man who can sort out the knottiest of technical problems swiftly and inexpensively. The kettle will always be on and they'll have plenty of time to discuss the pros and cons of a particular purchase. They're keen to let you try out as many things as you like for as long as you want, even if you're a fumble-fingered novice who only knows one excruciatingly boring riff. And they offer very affordable instrument tuition by a crack team of articulate, intelligent experts without any sales agenda at all.

We all know where this shop is, of course. It's in Narnia. Or somewhere else equally imaginary. But good shops certainly do exist, surviving even in these days of rocketing rents and crippling rates thanks to a faithful clientele, some sharp business acumen, a good site and a healthy dose of luck. It is certainly still possible to run across a real gem of a shop, even in the nest of vipers that is London's West End.

It would be nice to report that the bad ones have been driven out of business by them, but we all know that the world isn't fair like that; some fine places have gone under, while there are undeniably still scoundrels and scumbags in the trade, plus a fair few mediocre operators who struggle along, selling substandard stuff at inflated prices to people who know no better.

So how do you tell the righteous, respectable retailers from the rogues and rip-off ruffians? (Note: if this ever becomes an audiobook, I am intending to blow the entire budget on getting Jonathan Ross to read that sentence.)

People, as in most transactions, are the key. Any moron can stuff a few shiny guitars, amps and drums in a shop window and paint a name including the word 'rock' above it. But when you walk into the shop, how's their welcome? A smile, a word of greeting and an offer of help, or a blank stare? Or, most usual yet most irritating, total indifference?

It can't be that difficult for a shop owner to sit his staff down once in a while and instruct them to say hello to the customers. Some shops do this, and it makes a world of difference. Others, though, seem to be run by people who were once surly, offhand shop assistants themselves and know no other way of doing it.

The patronising youth is another staple of the bad music shop: their satisfaction seems to come almost entirely from making their little egos swell by vexing you in some condescending way. Whether it's totally ignoring you, disappearing mid-conversation to talk to somebody more interesting, or even picking up an instrument you've been trying out, then playing the same thing you were attempting, but faster and more flashily (yes, I have seen this done) they are the bane of any sensible instrument shopper's existence.

Other than arriving armed to the teeth and going on a serial killer-style rampage, which would be briefly satisfying but would seriously mess up your plan to have a quiet pint later, you have two forms of defence against Surly Youth. First, go over their head and talk to the manager/owner. If they're no better than their spotty employee, then I'm afraid it's down to direct action – simply refuse to buy anything from them, and go elsewhere for your gear.

There are plenty of ways to leave a snotty review online nowadays if they've been spectacularly irksome, but if they've just been lacklustre, unhelpful and limply useless it's probably best to quietly take your custom away. You won't be the only one, and that itself will hit them where it hurts – the till.

It's annoying if your local music shop is hopeless yet has a geographical monopoly by being the only one within miles, but these days distance is no barrier when it comes to new gear: the internet is your friend here (possibly). But we'll discuss that in the next bit.

What if your neighbourhood music shop is part of a chain rather than an independent? Actually, exactly the same thing applies. Sometimes the staff are stroppier, but in other cases they're actually more professionally trained. And as almost all of the people who work in music shops are skint musicians themselves, it's not as though you're going to be served by a spotlessly uniformed retail professional, whether it's at Alf's Accordions or GigaCorp RockStore Inc.; the talent pool they're all scrabbling for staff in is shallow, muddy and full of hairy, mumbly, slightly smelly young blokes. Well, not always blokes – the occasional girl braves the fug of testosterone and cheap deodorant, but in my experience they're not always more sympathetic. One lass who worked in an independent music shop of my acquaintance had a sneer that could peel the skin off an orange at 40 paces and delighted in terrifying customers clean out of the place. Predictably, that shop no longer exists.

Chain shops usually have some advantage on price thanks to the quantities they can buy in, often have a wider range of products thanks to their good relationships with importers, distributors and manufacturers, and in many cases will have a better-equipped test studio or soundproofed booth. They're good places to compare different bits of gear, but they tend to get very busy, particularly on Saturdays, when service may get especially offhand.

And there are also a fair few horror stories of after-sales care at some of the large chains turning into a nightmare of corporate miscommunication involving claims forwarded to Head Office, an outsourced warranty provider, a separate repair outfit, unreliable couriers, mislaid paperwork, and so on. Certainly when you decide where to buy that expensive and potentially unreliable bit of kit, it's worth thinking about how easy it will be to get it serviced, repaired or replaced in the event of trouble. Going to your local music shop and explaining the problem to a single human who will take care of it, and who can be chivvied or nagged personally, has a brutal simplicity to it.

Go to a big chain store by all means – many are very good. But make sure you're not swapping a few quid off the price for a lot of potential hassle.

Talking of the Saturday rush as we were, here's one nugget of wisdom that could make your shopping experience a lot more pleasant. If at all possible, go to a music shop when it's quiet; take a weekday morning off and have a relaxed twiddle on a few shiny bits of musical gear. The staff will be far more friendly, and you'll get longer to play with stuff. Also, you're much less likely to have some pint-sized twerp playing thrash-metal riffs at ear-bleeding volume three feet away.

It's certainly a good idea to avoid the post-school rush in many shops; four o'clock onwards becomes a hellish scene of pre-adolescent twiddling in many shops, so steer clear unless you really enjoy out-of-tune Guns N' Roses riffs and giggling.

Here's another dollop of music shop knowledge – if you want to get an idea of how good a shop is, take a close look at their stock. Are the guitars more or less in tune? Are the amps and keyboards plugged in and ready to play, or will that involve some huffing and a long, grumpy hunt for a working lead? Are the instruments clean, neatly racked or hung up, and recently dusted? Or is it a Steptoe & Son-style junkheap of precarious piles of dirty gear, waiting to collapse into an expensive mess if you go anywhere near it?

In short, do they give a stuff about their stock? If so, you can feel fairly confident that they're professional enough to be worth handing over some money to. But if they don't really care about what they're selling, odds are that they don't care about the people buying it either. And that's you.

There are a very few exceptions; occasionally you'll run across a shop that looks like a third-world jumble sale, with bits and pieces strewn everywhere and a general air of dilapidation. But in among the mess will be a few gems, and behind the counter will be a proudly eccentric old loon who knows absolutely everything about, say, Bakelite saxophones or 1950s British valve amplifiers or jazz drum kits. These places are to be treasured, and if you know exactly what you're after and how much it's worth you can sometimes turn up a good deal. But when it comes to buying new equipment, clean and tidy is almost always better.

Prices are a subject of much debate, both within the music industry and among the people who actually lay out their hard-earned wedge – us customers. Many manufacturers and distributors don't help themselves here (or us much either) by advertising their gear at a nominal retail price that is a work of fiction – nobody ever actually pays that price. How far below that price the item sells for is up to the individual retailer.

So your local independent music shop, which doesn't sell all that great a quantity of things, will probably try and make a reasonable margin, making their prices fairly high.

The big chain stores will likely get a better deal by buying a bigger quantity, so they'll be able to preserve their margin even when selling at a lower price. And they may be happy to cut their margin even further in return for increased turnover. So they'll be a bit cheaper.

And then we come to online retailers. They, of course, don't have to pay for shop premises, sales staff and all the other overheads. In some cases they don't place an order with the wholesaler until you've sent them your money, so they don't even need warehouse premises. So they'll be cheaper still. (But, beware of those delivery charges; they can start to add up alarmingly.)

So where do you buy? I must admit I like music shops, and I think an instrument is a physical, personal enough purchase to make it absolutely necessary to try out for yourself. You can't get the feel of a guitar's neck or a keyboard's action over the internet (yet). And a good music shop will always surprise you with something you hadn't considered or had a chance to try out in person – again, something the internet isn't good at.

But not everybody likes shopping, and particularly music shopping. Fair enough. The shop-shy, canny or cynical buyer will therefore go to a shop for the briefest amount of time necessary to try out something they like the look of, then go home and order it at the lowest price they can find online.

This is called 'showrooming' and it's the curse of retailers in all sorts of areas. It's been blamed for the downfall of high street giants like Game, Jessops and Comet, and it's hit retailers of mass-produced consumer goods very hard. If you're after, say, a new camera, you'll find deep discounts online, so you'll go to a shop only to see if it's comfortable to hold and looks as good as it did on the web. Then you'll buy it from the cheapest website you can find, knowing that when it arrives it'll be identical to the model you tested in the shop. The shop will be paying for the premises, the staff and the stock, yet making none of the money. Not a terribly successful business model at all.

Of course, this can come back and bite you on the bum when your cheap online purchase goes wrong, isn't what you expected, doesn't arrive, or turns out to be a forgery or a fake. Good luck trying to track down customer service if your retailer is in some obscure part of China and has changed web address three times in the last week.

That having been said, some of the more reputable online operators do have pretty slick after-sales backup, and some bricks-and-mortar shops also have their own online stores which offer the shop-phobic or housebound the piece of mind of a physical address and a phone number in case of problems.

Some of the more forward-thinking shops are also starting to offer an online price-matching promise. That's keen, verging on desperate, because it involves some major margin-slashing, but very attractive to the customer.

But bear in mind one other thing – any shop's price is just a number arrived at by some calculation, a bit of guesswork and a fair amount of wishful thinking. Whether you're in a tiny local shop or a giant retail warehouse, nobody minds if you ask whether there's any flexibility in the price. Haggle, my boy, haggle.

Even if the shop stands firm on their price, they're more than likely to sweeten the deal by throwing in a set of strings or sticks, a free strap or an extension on your warranty. And if you're reasonably determined and a good bargainer you might be surprised by how far down they'll move on a price.

Check the condition of your potential purchase carefully. Has it got a scratch or a knock? Are there signs of wear? Are there any small manufacturing defects like careless paintwork, misaligned knobs or excess glue on a joint or two? Does it have all the accessories – case, stand, box, all instructions, manufacturers' tags and paperwork?

If these things are important to you, go ahead and buy the immaculate example you're after, but don't expect a great deal of money off. But if you're actually not too bothered about small cosmetic imperfections or the lack of a case, and you find yourself looking at a mildly abused or shopworn bit of kit, you have a very good position from which to haggle yourself a decent discount.

Even if something's perfectly OK but has just been in the shop a long time, they may be keen to shift it to make room for new stock. If you've been walking past the same bit of rather unloved gear for many months, it might be ripe for a good deal to be struck. In the rather faddy world of guitars, for instance, most major manufacturers refresh their range at least once a year – usually just after the huge American NAMM trade show in January. That means that just after Christmas there'll be a fair few models that are about to be replaced, and therefore need to be cleared out cheapish.

In the ever-evolving world of technology the turnover is even more extreme. Nobody wants the TechnoThing 3.1 any more, as everybody knows the TechnoThing 3.2 is due out in a few weeks, and that's got 200 more gigawossits of memory and an adaptive USB wibbleiser as standard. So if you can stand being a version or two back from the bleeding edge of tech, you can pick up some perfectly functional gear for not much at all.

This is one area where it's well worth doing your homework. All the major magazines and websites will be making guesses of varying degrees of accuracy about what bits of gear are due to come out for several months before NAMM, and as soon as the show starts a flood of reports on new products gush out. The more wily retailers will know what they're getting well beforehand, but obviously want to keep selling stuff at full price for as long as possible, so they won't volunteer the information. However, if you go in to try a bit of kit knowing full well that it's about to be replaced by an updated or improved version, you have a very strong bargaining point. It might not be next year's model, but it could be a perfectly serviceable thing for a very good price.

Again, this is not something you can do on the internet. Trying to haggle with a computer is a fruitless task, as anyone who's seen *2001: A Space Odyssey* knows. First it says "I'm sorry, Dave, I can't do that", then it tries to blow you out of an airlock. Which is a bit unfriendly if you're just trying to get £10 off a drum stool.

There is, of course, another way to get a good deal out of a music shop, particularly a small, local independent one: be a regular. That doesn't mean you have to rush in twice a week to purchase a grand piano or equivalent, though; just pop in once in a while to say hello, see what they've got in stock and buy a few of the usual consumables – strings, sticks, batteries, leads and so on. If they see you as the sort of steady, pleasant customer they'd like to hang on to, you're much more likely to be offered that few extra quid off when something more costly comes up. And if you've seen something that you like online or in another shop, why not ask your local emporium if they can order it? They'll get a small profit, you'll cement your relationship, and they will almost certainly try to match the price you've seen it going for elsewhere if they can.

In case you think this is turning into a fanatical pro-music-shop rant, don't worry – there's absolutely nothing wrong with buying online. It's almost always cheaper and can be life-savingly convenient. But as the creaky old adage goes, you get what you pay for. Hopefully that's a shiny new instrument handed over with a smile, rather than a mis-delivered box of broken bits and a heap of hassle. To wheel out yet another ancient cliché, if it looks too good to be true, it probably is.

Be careful out there...

USED AND VINTAGE GEAR

What's the difference between used and vintage? As the old gag goes, about three zeros. But before we get into the intricacies of the classic kit market, let's begin with the basics.

A used piece of gear can be as simple and cheap as a well-thrashed item found in a local junk shop or a beaten-up hand-me-down from a mate, an older sibling or a kindly relative. It's what many of us started out playing on, and if you're learning an instrument it's usually the most cost-effective option.

But people do worry about older gear, of course. In the same way as some people buy a new car every three years just to have the comfort of a warranty and the security of thinking it won't break down, some players stick to brand new stuff because they believe it's going to be more reliable. But as anyone whose old banger has whizzed past a gleamingly new but decidedly broken-down car on the hard shoulder knows, it ain't necessarily so.

In general, the more mechanically and electrically simple a bit of gear is, the more likely it is to be a worthwhile second-hand buy. Guitars are on the whole amazingly sturdy things, and given a quick once-over by somebody knowledgeable, it's very easy to work out whether a used one is any good or not. Does it stay in tune? Is the action manageable? Do all the knobs and switches work, if it's an electric? That's more or less it.

Drums are equally obvious: stripped threads and wobbly stands are fixable or replaceable for not much outlay; if the basics are solid enough, you're fine. Wind instruments, even if often quite mechanically complex, can be assessed pretty straightforwardly, if time-consumingly, too just by trying all the levers, valves and/or keys.

More sophisticated electronics, however, start to get into the zone of guesswork and hope. Amplifiers are designed to be pretty rugged, though well-used knobs will start to get scratchy and, like any elderly relative, old amps can start to emit odd noises at inappropriate moments. But with most amps it's rare you'll run into something you can't live with or get fixed fairly cheaply.

Synthesisers, sequencers, drum machines and any gadgets with 'digital' in the title are considerably more risky. Not that there aren't experts who can fix most of the more popular bits of gear, but the all-in-one printed circuit board construction that's pretty much universal nowadays often means that mending one broken knob means effectively replacing the entire innards of the thing, which may well not be economically viable. So an only lightly damaged bit of gear goes off to landfill, and you traipse off to the shops to try and find another one. Boring.

But in all these areas there are bargains to be had, and buying used is a great opportunity to pick up an interesting item for a small amount of money, try it out and then, if it doesn't suit you, sell it again. If you buy wisely, you shouldn't lose much, if any, money on a deal and if you're knowledgeable or sharp you might even be able to subsidise your gear addiction by making a small profit. Ever wanted to try out a Peruvian nose flute, a bajo sexto or a concert harp? Give it a go and if it doesn't work out then release it back into the wild again for some other inquisitive musician to have a go at.

So where should you look for your second-hand stuff? Well, obviously there's your friendly (hopefully) local music shop. For more on the general pros and cons of that outlet see the New Gear section on page 125; but as far as used gear goes, music shops often have a reasonable selection of trade-ins, occasionally ex-rental or ex-demo kit, and other lightly thrashed bits and pieces. Prices can vary wildly from the extremely hopeful to the encouragingly realistic, depending on the whims of the owner/manager, the perceived saleability of any item, how well stocked their shelves are and any number of other factors including the prevailing wind direction, the position of Neptune in relation to Uranus and the price of chicken livers on the Shanghai market.

However, if you fancy something but it's a bit overpriced, there's nothing stopping you making an offer, or at least asking if a haggle's on the cards. And another fine tactic is patience. Just wait, and if that thing the manager assumed they'd sell quickly and expensively doesn't shift, the price will start to slide inexorably downwards. There's nothing like dusting a bit of gear twice a week for six months to make you keener to dispose of it.

Of course, there are many other places to find used gear. Junk shops, for instance – a bit of a dying breed these days, but once in a while something obscure and tatty will turn up. It may well need a bit of a clean, and often some technical fettling, but you could be lucky.

Charity shops are also a possibility; somewhere among the Catherine Cookson novels and beige tea sets you'll occasionally see an instrument that someone's found in Uncle Alf's attic. A lot of charity shops nowadays, however, are part of larger chains, and they employ people who know their merchandise. If a vintage gem arrived, it would fairly swiftly be hauled off to Head Office and auctioned at top prices.

Then there are the ever-expanding Cash Converters/ Cheque Converters-type pawnshop operations. There's always a slight moral wobble about buying from these places; a suspicion that you're somehow trading on someone else's misery. That gear probably isn't nicked or sold cheap by a desperate drug addict, and their payday loans at eye-watering interest are, strictly speaking, totally legal, but...

If you can overcome your scruples, though, it's undeniable that they do have rather random but often interesting stuff. It usually won't be in great condition, or terribly clean, and their guarantees are pretty skimpy, so make sure you try your new purchase out quickly. Prices vary wildly between a bit toppy and 'we've no idea what this is but we'll try it on anyway', and while they do attempt to check the price of everything on the internet a combination of untrained staff and a bit of a hurry can get you a bargain occasionally; mistaking Fenders for Squiers, mislabelling or just guessing the price can get you something for a random fraction of its true price. Or a multiple. Impossible to know which.

Then, of course, we come at last to that behemoth of tat, the gargantuan gorilla of second-hand goods – eBay.

There's no doubt that the auction site has hefty downsides. Anyone who's old enough to remember the pre-eBay era may have a rather rose-tinted image of all the things it's almost totally killed off – mystery finds in newspaper classifieds, car boot sale surprises, junk shops stuffed with underpriced gear, or just old-established music shops who'd long lost track of the modern value of their stock. Collectors would dine out on stories of remote, semi-mythical music shops full of sought-after items, still at 1965 prices; bands on tour, particularly in the USA, would place ads in local newspapers looking for vintage gear and often run across an elderly seller with a sad story of a son lost in Vietnam and an almost unplayed guitar under the bed which they'd let go for a few dollars. Cheap Trick's Rick Neilsen has a fabulous collection of almost priceless guitars, many acquired that way.

But of course those days ended when a would-be seller could go online and compare the price of almost anything with a couple of clicks, whether they happen to be in Leicestershire or Lexington, Nebraska, then find a buyer almost anywhere on the planet.

eBay has certainly had a levelling effect on prices – though that's not always a bad thing. In the same way as some shops underpriced their items, there were also some who had a grossly inflated idea of their value. An obscure 1970s Japanese widget known mainly for its incredible unreliability and peculiar name? That'll be £500 please. Oh no it won't – not nowadays, when 14 of the things have sold on eBay in the last six months for an average of £43.86. There are, of course, still people who put a desperately optimistic Buy-It-Now price on their online items, but renewing your listing every ten days for about a year must get very tedious.

Another huge leap forward is the range of gear that's now at your fingertips. Whatever you're looking for, someone somewhere will have one, in the colour you're after, and more likely there'll be several, vastly varying in condition and price.

It's created a busy market for smaller, less costly items like effects pedals, which some use as a buy-and-try scheme; if you buy wisely you can pick up something, give it a go for a while and if it doesn't work for you then just sell it on and use the proceeds to try an alternative. You've lost very little except the cost of postage, and you may have even made a small profit if you've got an eye for a bargain.

And if you've got some obscure bit of kit cluttering up your loft or spare room, eBay is a pretty decent way of getting rid of it. Whatever dusty relic you might be trying to dispose of, someone somewhere is probably looking for one. Just by sheer numbers, eBay has managed to become a way of marketing gear that you would have been stuck with for years before it came along.

Of course, whether you're buying or selling there are a few issues to consider – the cost and practicality of postage being one. If you're selling something small and lightweight, like the aforementioned effects pedals, the only matter you have to contend with is the queue of irritable old ladies armed with pointy-cornered trolleys in your local post office.

However, if you're saddled with disposing of a half-ton harmonium, your options are rather more limited. Location becomes a major issue here; if you're somewhere relatively central and easy to get to, there will be a pool of potential buyers who will probably not worry about collecting in person. On the other hand, if you're on a remote island or halfway down a goat track on a distant mountain-top your unwieldy item becomes a lot less attractive.

This can sometimes be a handy source of bargains, though. For reasons of logistical difficulty, lack of transport or sheer laziness, some buyers refuse point blank to send their item by post. Look for the 'collection only' tag, then check where they are. You may find that they're just down the road from you, or within easy reach of a friend or relative, but the lack of more far-flung bidders means that their item will usually end at some way below the usual price. In extreme cases, it'll go so cheaply that it leaves you enough money to pay for a courier service.

Couriers can be decidedly handy for those of us who don't have endless time to chase about all over the place – operations like ship.ly and MyHermes (google 'ebay couriers' – there are lots nowadays) can be very useful for both buyers and sellers, particularly if you're having a massive clearout and have a vast amount of stuff to send, when one pickup for multiple parcels can be arranged at a convenient time. Again, costs and availability will differ according to where you are.

This is where eBay stops being a pan-global resource and starts being dependent on geography again, so it's worth getting a few quotes to see if anyone's local to you and can do a good price.

And what about selling internationally? Again, it's a waste of time offering that bulky, heavy item to people in Guatemala and New Guinea as postage costs would be crippling, but for lightweight stuff it can make a lot of sense to widen your market, especially if what you've got is a little bit of a cult item. And while currency fluctuations make items from the UK relatively cheap for some nations, you may find a buyer from a better-off economy will think your gear is a complete bargain. Make absolutely sure you know how much postage is going to be, though, and beware of limitations – Australia, for instance, has a length limit on parcels, so that long-scale bass guitar might not actually be possible to send over there. Always get an accurate quote for the exact spot your bidder is from, not just a one-size-fits-all international cost. It can vary wildly, even within countries.

As a seller, you need to take heed of a few things. First, Italians. Not all Italians, to be fair – most are honest, trustworthy folk. But somewhere in their customs department, post office or elsewhere is a black hole which swallows parcels without a trace. eBay sellers have a vast number of horror stories about Italian buyers who never receive their items. Or is it that they claim never to have received them? Nobody knows. It's a huge cultural and national slur, but I'm going to hazard a guess that the Italian love of elegant disorganisation and charming chaos doesn't play nicely with the systematised, tidy systems of eBay and the like. Be a bit careful there.

Italy's by no means the only offender, though perhaps the most surprising; there are well-documented tales of eBay woe involving the ex-Eastern bloc countries, most central and west African nations, much of South America, Asia and the Indian subcontinent. It's possible to block certain countries from your selling preferences, but the old Latin phrase *caveat emptor* – let the buyer beware – also very much applies to sellers.

There are tales of scams galore, of course; some of which get stamped out by eBay itself, some that have become so common that nobody falls for them any more, and new ones that are being thought up by inventive criminals right now.

The more common tricks range from the very simple – claiming that an item hasn't been received, or selling non-existent goods – to the subtle and sophisticated, involving iffy money transfers, hijacking other people's pictures or whole listings, and particularly any sort of dodge that involves going off eBay entirely and trying to do a private deal.

However, there's a simple way to avoid these: don't be stupid. Engage your brain before pressing 'buy', sending money or posting anything. Think: What can go wrong? Does this feel right? Is this a little bit fishy? Is it too good to be true? (If so, it probably is.)

But while there are certainly dishonest people on eBay, they're a tiny minority. There are also other types of pond life: among these are the dreamers who bid on vastly expensive items (quite possibly while drunk) then don't complete the deal, leaving you to relist your item; the indecisive who decide they don't want your item after they've won it (you can't actually force someone to pay up); and the irritating quibblers who send endless questions about the item but never bid. But most people take the rough with the smooth, coming to the conclusion that its advantages outweigh its downsides.

Some people, though, utterly hate eBay. And you can see their point. In many ways, eBay doesn't help itself. As anyone who's tried to sort out a problem knows, communicating with eBay is like trying to have a meaningful conversation with a brick. Its company policy seems to be being blankly incommunicative, often giving the impression that they're deliberately ignoring you. Even if you do finally get hold of a human, they're very keen to throw you back into the system rather than sort out an issue.

Although the internet was once supposed to be a great way of communicating with people, it has actually made it very easy for firms to set up a great impersonal edifice with no human face whatsoever. Ever tried to get any sense out of Amazon? YouTube? Google? You can't.

Also, if you do get thoroughly fed up with eBay and decide to use alternative methods of buying and selling, you find out that almost all of them are actually owned by the auction giant. An ad on Gumtree? Owned by eBay. Selling site Yakaz? eBay. Preloved? eBay. And so on. A bit dispiriting.

Then there's the company's strategy of veering further and further towards Amazon as an avenue for large retailers and manufacturers to sell multiple goods. While they're courting the likes of Dixons and Top Shop, it would be easy to feel that the small private seller is being ignored, if not actively discriminated against. Although the company's roots lie in simple person-to-person transactions (famously, if dubiously, starting with fans of Beanie Babies), its business expansion plans long outgrew the sort of revenue that is attainable through hobbyists and collectors. They want the big bucks, and sometimes as a private customer it feels like you're in the way of that.

More reasons to dislike eBay include its own payments system, PayPal, which is run on similar, if not even more opaque, lines to its parent company. Yes, it is possible to get a refund if you use PayPal for a transaction that goes awry, but if anything more complex happens, they're decidedly elusive. It is pushed hard as the default payment system for eBay, simply because if you use it they effectively get paid twice. Cunning.

And talking of PayPal, there are those fees. If you've sold a lot of stuff, the size of the invoice that pops up a few weeks later can come as a horrible shock. While individual elements of a selling price, like adding extra pictures or international listing, don't seem to be that costly, the total can come to a fair chunk of the final value.

When you're considering whether to accept that fairly low offer from a mate, or a mildly insulting part-exchange deal from a local shop, try to bear that in mind. The final selling price may look higher, but when you count in postal hassle and fees, it might not be as hugely profitable as it looks.

So is it worth it? With a few reservations, yes. eBay has become the default place to buy used gear, and you can find pretty much anything you want on there, even if you're forced to compete with other would-be buyers for it. And if you've got something to sell, you'll find someone who wants it, even if you have to tangle it up in 300 yards of bubblewrap and lug it to the post office.

CHAPTER 7

ERASE/REWIND

Gigging's good. No doubt about it, that's what many musicians live for. But it's by no means all there is to making music. And if you don't fancy it, you don't have to do it at all; you can have a perfectly satisfying and absorbing time without ever going near a stage. This is where recording comes in.

Of course, if you are a gigging band or artist, the process of getting some music recorded is a necessary thing too, if only to get some evidence of your style and talent to show potential bookers what you're all about.

But if you're more of a considered, intellectual type than a noisy show-off, you might well find the possibilities and intricacies of recording far more up your street than sweating your bits off on a stage. The process of layering tracks one by one to form a cleverly interlocking whole is something that can take a lifetime to really master; if you get into recording you'll never be short of tricks to learn, ideas to experiment with or technical advances to get up to speed on.

The gear itself covers a vastly wide area, from arcane valve-driven relics that Elvis would have recognised to software-based digital audio packages that squeeze a fully equipped studio into your iPad. You can combine them in innovative ways, finding new uses for old classics or mixing analogue and digital to create a distinctive sound of your own.

Given a decent selection of software instruments and a talent for linking them together, there's no need to get a 'real' instrument involved at all. Time can be stretched and squeezed, frequencies can be swapped, tunings altered at will. If you can imagine it, the chances are that you can achieve it. A dubstep concerto for supermarket till bleeps? Easy.

Or you can step out of the way entirely and aim for a clear, transparent and true reproduction of natural sounds. Getting an acoustic instrument to sound good when recorded should be the easiest thing in the world, but in reality it's amazingly complicated and tricky, with tiny changes in microphone positioning or acoustic baffling making a huge difference to the end result. Knowing how to get a voice or an instrument to leap out of the speakers sounding fresh and natural is one of the biggest challenges of all.

So get into that studio and rattle those pots and faders. Whether it's a purpose-built multitrack palace or your back bedroom and a laptop, recording's a whole new musical world.

DOING IT AT HOME

Once upon a time, having a recording studio at home was strictly for rock stars and other music-obsessed millionaires. Now, all the equipment you need to capture and process a decent-quality recording is your phone. Next time somebody moans about ever-increasing inequality, you could mention that as a good example of the opposite. Just before they push you under the wheels of a passing banker's speeding Lamborghini, of course.

It's true that recording technology has moved on hugely. But the main thing that's given to us is choice. It's entirely possible to pack a perfectly usable professional studio's worth of recording tech on to a laptop and a couple of plug-in boxes. The recording software packages (often referred to as DAWs – Digital Audio Workstations) that are available nowadays are simply awesome. One of the simplest, though still very capable, is Apple's Garageband. You could record a perfectly decent album on this, and people have. It works on an iPad or even an iPhone, and looks utterly lovely. Or you can plunge headlong into the professional world of packages like Logic and ProTools, which are incredibly powerful but have a steep learning curve. Luckily, there's a vast array of tuition videos, user forums and other help available if and when you get stuck. There's also a whole world of software plug-ins, ranging from realistic guitar effects pedal simulators to brass sections, orchestral sounds or complex, fully editable rhythm tracks. It's the state of the art in current recording, used by everybody from top professionals to school pupils.

But the luxury of an old-school mixer with separate, accessible channels, and some all-analogue effects with their inherent warmth and character, is still something many recording enthusiasts aim for. And then there's the simple fact that unless you're recording all-digital instruments you'll need a certain amount of room for the people who make the noise, whether that's a vocal booth, a drum room or enough space for that 120-piece orchestra you think might add a little class to your demo.

So if you're thinking of setting up your own Abbey Road, the first thing to think about is where. Got a spare room? This might work. Basements, if there's enough headroom, are good. A garage, shed or other outbuilding? Maybe.

But if you're intending to record live instruments, or listen to mixes on proper (loud) monitor speakers, bear in mind that you'll be generating a fair amount of racket. Unless you live alone in an isolated detached house (or, of course, are warden of the Lundy Island Home for the Deaf) you'll need to think about the other inhabitants of your house and your neighbours. Vibration, particularly bass notes, can travel a long way, and if you're thinking of continuing your sessions deep into the night you may get complaints from a surprising distance away.

The posh, and fiercely expensive, answer to this is to build an isolated room; a custom-built floor suspended on blocks of rubber, bespoke internal walls floating away from the main structure, double-skinned doors and everything covered in a thick layer of sound-absorbing and sound-deadening insulation. This will work. This will also cost a fortune, but if you're serious and moneyed it's the way to go.

The rest of us will have to be a little more DIY about the whole thing. The floating floor idea isn't a bad one; you could knock up something vaguely similar from polystyrene insulation and cheap tongue-and-groove floorboards – the internet's full of plans ranging from ultra-complex to lash-up. A quick Google will give you plenty of ideas.

As for the walls, how about egg boxes? No, not really.

This was at one time a DIY studio staple; the idea was that they formed cheap baffles to deflect and dampen high frequencies, which they more or less did. But these days foam panels are available, which aren't terribly expensive and do the same sort of job but much more efficiently and easily. By the time you've eaten enough eggs to give you terminal constipation and spent hours with sticky tape and staples trying to put them up, you might as well have just bought some cheap panels. Still, if you want your studio to look like a very early, inferior Doctor Who set, egg boxes are by far the best way to go.

There are two major weak points in any home studio design – windows and doors. A room without windows is more like a cell, but they do leak sound very efficiently outwards, and reflect it inwards. And assuming your middle name isn't Houdini, you'll need a door of some sort. The windows may have to be sacrificed for the greater good. It's lovely to sit listening to your tracks at enormous volume while looking out at the garden, but if there's anybody within 200 yards of said garden they'll be less impressed when their birdsong is blotted out by your bassline.

Basements and cellars are good from that point of view, provided they've got reasonable headroom and aren't too dank and smelly. They're already insulated by the surrounding earth, and their windows are small or non-existent. If you can ensure sufficient ventilation and dry warmth with vents, fans and heaters (audio gear doesn't work too well when it gets damp) then they're pretty good. You may have to reverse the floating floor principle and build some insulation into the ceiling of your subterranean lair to avoid too many vibrations working their way up and out, but in general going underground (as recommended by The Jam) is a good option.

Garages, sheds and barns have their own charm – if they're a good distance from any habitation they can be almost perfect. Though you then have possible issues with power, but let's assume that they're already equipped with electricity. They do usually have thin walls and roofs, however, so if it's likely to get unsociably loud then some serious insulation work will have to occur. Bear in mind, too, that this can reduce your available space quite drastically. Some sheds and garages aren't terribly roomy to start with, so subtracting six or eight inches in every direction might leave you a bit tight on elbow room.

If you've got a stone-built barn, a roomy brick garage or some other sturdy structure, you're laughing. Lighthouses, brick kilns, small castles and sea forts are also highly recommended, if annoyingly uncommon.

So now you've got a dry, warm, roomy and well-insulated studio to work in, what gear do you need in there? Bit of a 'how long is a piece of string' question, this. You know what kind of thing you want to record, and that will largely determine the kind of kit you need. If you're all-electronica, then your bleeps and bloops could be served perfectly well by a mixing desk and a powerful computer. Though a wall of huge, complex and cronky vintage analogue synthesisers would, of course, add that vital finishing touch to the decor.

If you're intending to record real instruments, your needs are more wide-ranging. If you're mostly doing electric guitars, there are some very convincing software packages or plug-in amp emulators that will get you the 'wall of stacks' effect without the associated earache. Bass can plug more or less straight into the desk, ditto keyboards.

Vocals are fairly straightforward – the finer points of getting a good vocal recording are the subject of much debate, and some producers have spent their entire careers trying to perfect the art, but at its most basic it's about a decent microphone and a room that sounds neutral enough not to interfere with the sound. Even the most excitable blues shouter doesn't produce a huge amount of volume compared to drums or most amplified electric instruments, so your insulation needs aren't enormous.

Most acoustic instruments are more or less along the same lines; having enough room to play with mic positioning or adjust a movable baffle or two to minimise unwanted reflections is nice, but again you shouldn't need to go mad with the soundproofing.

Drums, though, are where your problems start. There's an old joke that runs like this. A: What's the difference between a drummer and a drum machine? Q: With a drum machine, you only need to punch in the instructions once. Sorry, drummers. But it's not accurate anyway – there's another difference. Volume.

An acoustic drum kit produces a fearsome amount of racket, which causes issues in all sort of areas. Firstly, insulation, neighbours and external noise. Secondly, echoes and reverberations inside the studio itself. And thirdly, leakage into anything else you're trying to record at the same time.

They're a nightmare to record. They need a large amount of room, a huge amount of microphones and a vast amount of time and patience to get sounding decent. But that having been said, however good your programming technique, a good drummer can add excitement and movement to a track in a unique way. They can be a nuisance, but they're a necessary and usually music-enhancing one, so get over it.

Recording a whole band all at once is a job for a seriously large studio. Yes, it's certainly possible to squeeze a drum kit into the kitchen, the singer into a nice echoey bathroom and spread amps and microphones all over the rest of the house, but if you haven't got that luxury (or about 500 yards of cabling) then you'll have to record the band separately, in tidy chunks, or do it elsewhere. Handily, there's a bit on that 'elsewhere' option in a few pages' time.

Even if you stick to a minimal instrumental set-up, you'll still have to find room for all the required bits of recording gear that you'll need. A decent-sized mixing desk is pretty much essential, and one with enough ins and outs for all the stuff you might want to stick through it. If you're recording to digital, as almost everybody does these days, you'll need to find room for a good-sized screen plus the computer itself, keyboard and mouse. A patchbay for all those ins and outs, plus somewhere to hang the necessary leads. Somewhere to put mikes and stands when not in use. Then there's the inevitable rack of recording-related odds and sods – reverbs, compressors, limiters, amp emulators, mic pre-amps and other shiny things with blinking lights.

Is it starting to feel a bit crowded yet? It should be.

To bring it down to a decidedly non rock 'n' roll level, a working studio actually takes up much the same space as a kitchen, complete with worktops, sink, fridge and cooker. So when you're working out if you can squeeze a studio under the stairs or in the pantry, try to aim for a bit more space than you think you'll need.

Also, remember that once you get keen you'll find that gear somehow accumulates. Do you really need that lovely bit of valve-driven ex-BBC kit with Bakelite knobs and big impressive meters on the front? No. Is it going to make a vast improvement to your recorded results? No. Will you buy it anyway? Yes.

And if you're going down the old-school tape-recorder route, even if just a two-track machine to bounce things down to, that's a large amount more space you'll need. Suddenly that spacious spare room is a cramped, gear-filled nest of wires and widgets. Do try to consider tidy wiring when you're planning a studio too – having mains adaptors, extensions and signal leads all tangled together and sprawling across every surface is a recipe for disasters of all kinds, from interference to a rather inconvenient house fire. Now that really would make you unpopular with the neighbours if you live in a semi.

And once you've got it all installed and plugged in, you'll find out that your hermetically sealed, perfectly soundproof room has one major disadvantage – it's stuffy. Equipment puts out a surprising amount of heat; once everything's on and working hard it's like switching on a three-bar electric fire. Sitting in your pants dripping sweat onto the desk is neither glamorous nor efficient, so you have to consider some sort of ventilation. A powerful electric fan is a basic bodge, but doesn't really solve the problem and can add unwanted noise, vibration and electrical interference to the situation. You'll need some way of dispersing heat without allowing noise out, which is tricky at best. Small fan-assisted vents (Xpelair and the like) can help a little; if it gets seriously sweaty, though, a small air-conditioning unit might come in handy. Just make sure it runs quietly and smoothly, though; having something that rumbles, hisses or switches itself off and on with juddering thuds defeats the object, as you'll have to turn it off any time you're actually recording.

Yet another thing to think about is power. This isn't something you normally take much notice of, but if you're planning a studio then you've got to take account of a few vital points. Firstly, is there any? Sheds, garages and outbuildings might need wiring up from scratch (more on that later).

Secondly, how much is there? Some recording gear pulls a large amount of current, then there are heaters, fans, air-con or whatever else you're using to keep comfortable. A kettle's a nice idea, but that can eat up your amps too. Make sure you've got a decent amount of power on tap, and that it's coming through fairly recent and well-insulated wiring.

And thirdly, how clean is it? Many bits of high-end recording equipment are quite finicky about their voltage. Electrical interference, brownouts (where power drops below the usual voltage) and other nasty and difficult-to-diagnose problems can all be the result of a dodgy power supply.

If you run into problems, or you want to avoid

them in the future, the first port of call is probably an electrician. Running a separate line from the fusebox is an expert job but it shouldn't be too expensive, and that way you'll make sure that it's decent quality, unconnected to any other sources of trouble, and will feed you enough amps. Mystery clicks or buzzes can drive you absolutely mental, whether it's old Gladys next door switching on her bathroom light, your freezer turning itself off or the security light over the back porch being triggered by a passing squirrel, so do everything you can to bypass any possible issues.

Another option is to run everything from a good-quality isolated power supply unit of the sort that computer servers are connected to. If you want one that passes a fair amount of power it won't be terribly cheap, but what price peace of mind? Or just live with it. Click. Bzzzzzz. Phzt. Arrggh.

So having found a decent-sized space, insulated it well, vented it, heated it, wired it up properly and filled it with good-quality, well-maintained gear, connected together neatly and laid out comfortably, what then?

That bit's up to you. Concept album or punk demo? Electronic soundscapes or rootsy acoustic recordings? Or all of the above? Your choice. Have fun with it and, if you're going for that vintage Abbey Road vibe, remember not to get your tie caught in the tape reels.

IN A PRO STUDIO

This always, somehow, makes you feel like a 'proper' musician. When somebody asks you what you're doing at the weekend and you reply, "Oh, I'm going into the studio", that statement comes with metric tons of unspoken baggage like "...to record a best-selling double album" or "...to put down a hit single" or just "...to have a fistfight with the drummer, take shedloads of drugs and vomit over the mixing desk". Well, maybe not that last one, unless you're a member of Mötley Crüe. In which case, how come you're still alive and reading a book? Are there no groupies left to ravage and no drugs left to take? Get back to work immediately.

It must take a very jaded pro musician not to feel a little trickle of excitement at the opportunity to have your songs immortalised, your playing flattered and occasionally even your ego massaged in a professional recording studio.

It also comes with a slight edge of nervousness. Once the red light goes on, there's nowhere to hide. That note you always fluff at the end of the solo; that chord you always play quietly because you never bothered to learn quite what it was; that dodgy downbeat into the bridge that you never quite get right – all these things can be fudged around and lost in the noise and excitement of a gig, but once you're in the studio your parts are under the microscope.

Which brings us to the first rule of a successful recording session – almost all the work needs to be done before you go anywhere near the studio.

So let's go through the process. This is universal; it doesn't matter whether you're booked in for three months at the hottest studio in New York or a half-day with a mate who's got a four-track cassette recorder. Here's what you have to do.

First, make a plan. What do you want to record, and why?

If you're doing a straightforward demo purely in order to get gigs, you won't need many songs. Three or four, probably; just enough to let any prospective bookers get an idea of what you do. You may want to put more songs down if you're doing a CD to sell at gigs or online; you may be documenting an entire career's worth of material for posterity.

This obviously determines how long you'll need to book in a studio. A three-minute song will not take three minutes to record. With getting a sound, fluffed takes and overdubs, three hours would be very good going. And then not a lot less to mix it down to a decent standard. Take that into account. If in doubt, ask the engineer at a potential studio or two, or some recording-savvy mates.

Also, how complicated is your material? And how many musicians are involved? All of those things will have an effect on how long you'll need to spend recording and mixing. So think about what you wish to do, and allocate enough time to get it all done comfortably.

Do you need to do recording and mixing at the same time? It's often a good idea to split them up; record your songs in one session, get some rough mixes done, then take them away and listen to them a few times. You can come back a week or so later with fresh ears and having had a chance to talk about how it should sound, which will make the process smoother.

Unless you own a professional studio, this is a very good time to do some recording. Thanks largely to the availability of low-budget, high-quality software recording set-ups, many of the pro studios have suffered badly in recent years and are therefore offering very decent deals indeed. You can get a day's recording, with an engineer, for £100 or so. This wouldn't have bought an hour in many of those places not too long ago. So there's no need to skimp on time unless you're utterly skint.

Don't try to pack too many tracks into your allotted time, either. Unless you find you've achieved absolute perfection and still have four hours left (highly unlikely), stick to your plan and polish the songs you've decided to do. Are you sure there isn't a better take to be done on a part? Are you certain that it sounds as good as possible? In recording, it's all about the details. Make sure they're as faultless as can be rather than crash on and produce rushed, sloppy results.

Your pre-studio routine should also include the other kind of studio – the rehearsal studio. Decide on the songs you're doing, then block out several rehearsals to work on just those ones; get them absolutely 100% tight and polished, make sure everybody knows exactly what they're doing at all times, and pull them apart to be certain that the arrangements are cast iron and committed to memory. The recording studio is not a good place to rehearse or rearrange. The clock is ticking and the important decisions should all have been made well beforehand, leaving only the crucial, and difficult, job of getting a great performance in unfamiliar surroundings.

Which surroundings? Obviously you'll choose a studio largely depending on your musical style and set-up – a 16-piece brass ensemble may not pick the same studio as a synth-pop duo – but if there's a choice then do a bit of homework. Do you know any musicians who've used a studio? Can they recommend it, or possibly advise that you not bother? Most studios' websites contain a list of clients – look through it for bands or artists that are in a similar vein to you. See if there are any samples available to listen to. And if it's a one-man operation, as so many are, ring up and have a chat with the owner/engineer and find out what sort of music they like, what instrument they play themselves, and what the facilities are like for your sort of set-up. Do they have a good drum room or booth? Are they used to recording noisy guitar bands or will you find yourself trying to play at an unfamiliar hushed volume because they've got neighbour issues? Conversely, can they handle an acoustic outfit, or do they just specialise in electronic music?

And make sure you do all this planning well in advance. Booking a studio just because you've left it to the last minute and it's the only one available the weekend you can all make it is a deeply hit-and-miss arrangement.

You'll find when you do get into the studio, unless you're an experienced hand, that it's all a bit alien. You may want to sound just as thrilling as you do live, but the process of getting to that point could well involve recording each part separately and adding in all sorts of processing, just to arrive back where you started. Or that's what it seems like – in fact, what you think you sound like probably isn't actually how you sound at all. If you can construe that somewhat tangled sentence, well done. But what it means in reality is that the process of recording sometimes seems counterintuitive; you don't necessarily take the most direct route to the best sound. That will surprise you. So will things like playing or singing in headphones, trying to get excited in an acoustically dead and visually boring room on your own, and getting a sound that you don't actually like on the promise that 'it'll fit much better in the mix'.

All of these are part of the process, and all are good reasons why you should be rehearsed to the point of being able to play your parts in your sleep. When all these other factors are confusing and confounding you, being able to pull out a decent performance becomes a very useful thing to fall back on.

You should also have used some of your pre-studio time to discuss precisely what you're aiming for. If you've got a specific artist in mind whose sound you admire, that's often a good thing. Don't worry, you won't be sued for plagiarism if you try to replicate the character of a much-admired star's recordings. In fact, it's unlikely you'll even come close, but it's good to have a general direction agreed. And it's no bad thing to send a few tracks to the engineer of your chosen studio anyway, to see if they think it's something they could attempt and give them an idea of what you're aiming for.

Agreement is vital anyway. While studios are bad places to rehearse or rethink material, they're even worse places to have an argument about it. Tensions can be high when the pressure is on to get a good result; time is tight and you're paying your own money, so things can get a bit tetchy. Try to cover all those potential points of conflict well beforehand

and achieve some compromises. If each member of a band is determined that their part will be louder than everybody else's it's not going to end well. Remember that an engineer is there to set up gear, twiddle knobs and get you sounding half-decent, not to act as a United Nations peace envoy when it all kicks off.

And don't forget to take all those spares you'd take to a gig. Strings, sticks, leads, batteries, the usual stuff. Some studios keep a stock of these essentials, many don't. Half-past nine on a Sunday night, at a studio smack in the middle of an out-of-town industrial estate, is not a good time to suddenly snap a top E string if you don't have a spare.

Talking of half-past nine, try to set sensible recording hours. Yes, the Rolling Stones recorded *Exile on Main Street* in sessions that only started when their semi-nocturnal legend Keith Richards was awake, so usually from about 2am onwards. But they were used to those hours. Unless you continuously work night shifts, you're not.

So try to start at a realistic hour in the morning, make sure everybody turns up on time, and even if you're having a great time, try not to go on too late. You'll be knackered and ratty, the engineer will be too, and your ears will be fatigued by listening to the same parts over and over again. Don't take any important decisions late at night after a long day – save it until you're fresher, even if that means booking another few hours to finish a tricky mix.

But all those warnings aside, a recording session is a great chance to hear what you really sound like, to listen back to your own playing enhanced by some subtle effects, and to come out with a result that makes you sound better than you'd hoped. When you play a track to someone and they say "Is that actually you? It sounds really professional" then it's job done; your ego gets a much-needed stroke and it's all been worthwhile. Also, you'll find that the process of exhaustively recording a set of songs will make you play them much better live, and you'll find yourself trying to drag the rest of your set up to that standard. It can really improve your sound.

It's also addictive; the interestingly different discipline of the studio, the adrenalin rush of doing a perfect take and the chance to emerge with a concrete result is something you can easily find yourself wanting to indulge in again and again. Just don't forget to pop outside once in a while. They don't call it a studio tan for nothing.

RECORDING LIVE

Sometimes, you don't need the fine art of a proper studio – you just want the rough sketchpad scribble of a live, or rehearsal, recording.

But just because it's a bit rough and ready doesn't mean it should sound like someone's mobile ring tone being played through a box of Rice Krispies. There are a few ways to go about getting a reasonably decent sound which don't involve a mobile studio built into a large lorry and 14 miles of cable.

First, let's talk about what you need, and why. For most live purposes, you don't need to record on to multitrack; stereo's plenty. Luckily, there are now loads of affordable, purpose-designed digital stereo recorders that are designed specifically for recording live music. Zoom is one popular make; Line6 also make them, and there are plenty more – a quick online search will pop up heaps of alternatives. Most of these are simple two-microphone battery-operated gadgets, often with a screw socket on the bottom for a mike stand. Set them up, press record, hey presto. Some will even do video, so if you want to watch yourself prancing about embarrassingly, then upload it to YouTube for others' amusement, off you go.

You take them home, hook them up to your computer and download the files to listen to, send to other band members, or in some cases instantly delete out of excruciating shame. This should be quick, easy and surprisingly good quality.

A couple of warnings, though – some of these take the idea of digital one-button simplicity to extremes, and doing anything other than the very basic functions can be a nightmare of intricate menus on a tiny screen and multiple presses of fiddly buttons. Read a few online reviews before you take the plunge, as trying to set up one of the less user-friendly models in a dimly lit rehearsal room will drive you bonkers. And make sure that it records files in a fairly common format like MP3 or MP4; it's not unknown for recorders to use their own software which won't run on all computers and doesn't play well with others.

On to rehearsal recording then. Taking a snapshot of what you're up to at rehearsals can be invaluable for checking progress, assessing whether new material's working or analysing arrangements.

If you rehearse, as most do, organised in a rough

circle facing inwards, then the logical position for a recorder is in the centre. You might think that anyway, but it's not always the case; the peculiarities of acoustics mean that you'll have to experiment a bit. The best location might actually be behind the bass amp, under the drummer's jumper. Record a track, then listen back and see what the balance is like. Don't forget your headphones – it's the best way to get an accurate feel of the results. Plugging your recorder into the PA to listen back will introduce all sorts of potential variables to the sound. Fine if you want everybody to have a quick, rough listen to what's going on but if you're trying to get a well-balanced sound initially then decent headphones are the way to go.

Sometimes you'll have to change the way you arrange yourselves; lining up as if on stage, with the recorder placed centrally, should give you a good stereo image. Watch out for reflective surfaces behind the band or the recorder, though – a big mirror or flat, hard wall will introduce echoes that will blur your sound. Try setting up at a slight diagonal to any flat walls, so the sound doesn't ping-pong straight off them.

One further warning – with many recorders' vast amount of digital memory, it's easy to record a whole rehearsal. This will take you several hours to listen back to (including an awful lot of meaningless chat, clanking of drum stands, fiddling with guitar pedals, etc etc) and once you've done that a few times you'll also end up with megabytes of unnecessary rubbish clogging up your computer and an aching finger where you've been pressing fast forward. Be sparing; when you think you've got a track in recordable form, let everybody know that it's being recorded, and play it as though you were live. Straight through, start to finish, as well as you can. Then you'll get an idea of what it sounds like, rather than a ramshackle thrash when nobody's really concentrating.

With a bit of practice, you can get amazingly good results out of one of those portable recorders. You might even be able to use it as a demo if you get the balance more or less right and do a little editing later.

Or you could try and record yourselves live. This could be a bit more involved, depending on whether you want to come away with a multitrack recording to be mixed later, or just a half-decent stereo document of a gig. Some venues offer this service to bands anyway, for a few quid, and if they're experienced at doing it then it can be well worth the outlay. Otherwise it's a matter of talking to the engineer to see if they're OK with you taking a feed from the mixing desk. If you're just grabbing a stereo output with a portable recorder, they'll usually be fine with it. Taking a multitrack output, though, is much more complicated and would usually need some prearrangement with the management and a few hours wiring everything up, setting levels and maybe adding a few extra mikes to capture audience noises and atmosphere. This is a case where bringing in your own engineer would make an awful lot of sense.

In many larger venues pretty much everything goes through the desk; their soundman will be watching levels, adding effects and trying to get a decent balance throughout, so what you'll get from your stereo recording should be a half-decent mix. The quieter you play on stage, the less will bleed out over the PA and the better your mix will be, so bear that in mind.

Smaller venues, however, may not be as straightforward. They might not have the bass, guitars or all of the drum kit miked up; they may just have bass drum and snare, for instance. In this case your mix from the desk will be incomplete and weirdly balanced – you're better off putting a portable recorder at the back of the venue.

If you do that, or leave one plugged into the desk, try to make sure there's somebody keeping an eye on it during your set. Engineers are busy people; if they turn away for a moment to fiddle with an equaliser or something it's all too easy for some scumbag to quietly unplug and snaffle your expensive recorder. Likewise, if you leave it somewhere visible yet unattended it's easy meat for the light-fingered. Be careful out there.

But do record yourself, and do it often enough to spot flaws in your sound, see where you're heading in the right direction or hear where you're going down a musical blind alley. It's dead straightforward to send recordings to the rest of the band, or upload them somewhere (Soundcloud, Dropbox or Google Drive are three favourites) and send a link round so everybody can listen and come back with ideas or comments. Technology? Isn't it marvellous! Oh hang on, my computer's cra

CHAPTER 8

YOU WEAR IT WELL

Rock 'n' roll, according to the accepted wisdom, is a young person's game. It's all about pretty seven-stone teenagers with washboard stomachs and unblemished complexions. Well, frankly, this is cobblers. That line of thinking takes you down a horrible path that leads to Little Jimmy Osmond, Justin Bieber and any amount of pouty, idiotic boy bands.

There is still a general assumption that the older you get, the more ridiculous you look on stage. This is simply not true – or it doesn't have to be.

Yes, you're not as young as you were. But then nobody is. It's a reasonable guess that if you're reading this you've got a fair number of birthdays notched up, but this is not a problem. Particularly if your audience is also a little more mature than the average teenybopper.

Once you attain a certain maturity as a musician, you do have to take a little more care over your personal appearance, your onstage demeanour and your choice of clobber. But that's as true offstage as on. It's not that difficult to swap from carelessly sloppy yoof styling to something with a little more dignity, gravitas and timeless cool. You just have to give it a few minutes' thought.

And one thing that helps a great deal is the confidence that you gain with age. As a callow youngster, you no doubt bravely exclaimed "I don't care what anybody thinks!" while casting anxious glances in all directions to see what everybody was thinking. As you get on a bit, though, you gain the ability to really not care what anyone thinks and to just get on with the job in hand. Confidence and poise come with that attitude, and that's something to be exploited.

You may not be interested in dancing like a frantic gibbon these days, but is that such a bad thing? No. Swap your sweaty lunacy for a bit of suave cool, and you'll start to get regarded as a living legend instead of a raving nutcase.

Think of a few more mature musicians who are still packing them in. Van Morrison: barely moves. Leonard Cohen: occasionally doffs his trilby. Dr John: sits down. Eric Clapton: sometimes moves his left elbow slightly.

Yes, Mick Jagger is still doing that electrocuted chicken dance on stage. But isn't it more than a bit embarrassing? Has the man no idea of how he looks? Actually, if you're Mick Jagger, there's probably nobody who dares to tell you that you shouldn't be shaking your fragile hips quite so violently these days.

No, age-appropriate stagecraft is the way to go. Show those young whippersnappers that it's not all about who can leap the highest, it's about who can look the coolest. And however much they run, jump and pout, that could well be you.

COOL OR NOT?

You know the sort of music you play. And unless it's hardcore dubstep, it's probably been around for quite a while. There will be some history behind it, a good few legendary figures, an established style and a rough dress code.

That dress code is, of course, often used as shorthand, and quite often not in an entirely complimentary way. For instance, when you think of a particular form of music, there's often one item of clothing that's used to sum it up. Jazz = beret. American rock = blue jeans. Rural blues = dungarees. Urban blues = suit. Country = stetson. Lounge = tuxedo. Funk = flares. Folk = woolly jumper. Heavy metal = leather trousers. And so on.

You are, naturally, completely at liberty to ignore these off-the-cuff categorisations. Nobody's going to haul you off to jail for playing country and western in a lounge suit. Though perhaps the leather trousers should be a punishable offence unless you're a German Harley-Davidson owner.

But they can be helpful. Apart from being a sort of visual cue that lets people know what they're about to hear, it also marks you out as a member of the right sort of club; one of the in crowd. And if what you choose to wear is a definite statement, it also says that you've gone to the trouble of taking it a bit seriously.

To a large extent, all of these genre stereotypes have come into existence as a result of being a trend at one time or another.

The way trends work, undoubtedly, is a continual series of actions and reactions. Trends and anti-trends, if you like. A good example is Nirvana and the other Seattle grunge puppies, who may have looked like they crawled out of bed and slung on the first thing they found, but were actually putting on a well-thought-out anti-rock star image. They wanted to look different to the rock clichés of the previous generations like Kiss and Black Sabbath. Rebels in a woolly check shirt? Why not? And of course within months of them being successful, legions of followers were putting on the Seattle slacker uniform. Not long afterwards, the pendulum swung back the other way with The White Stripes and their incredibly controlled, tidy, colour-co-ordinated image. And so it goes.

Musicians define themselves by their clothing, not just in terms of what they are, but of what they're not. So wearing the 'right' sort of thing gives an audience some sort of comfort that you're on their side and share the same likes and dislikes. Hence, turning up to your earnest progressive jazz quartet's gig dressed in a purple, flared sparkly jumpsuit in the style of The Stylistics might, just, not actually get you thumped in the nose by a trombonist, but it'll set enough people's teeth on edge to make your gig a slightly uncomfortable experience. Unless you're aiming for comedy progressive jazz, of course, in which case I wish you the best of luck in your microscopic sub-niche. I still won't be coming to see you very often.

So embrace those clichés. Use them as a starting point or as basic, if vague, guidance. Subvert them a little if you like, but don't pretend they don't exist; they're useful.

And more importantly, don't just turn up to play in your gardening clothes. Jeans and a T-shirt are comfortable, unchallenging and don't require much thought. They're also dull, lazy and disappointing. Get a grip. There's a reason why a stage is built off the ground instead of in a hole – people want to look at you. So you might as well make it worth their while and give them something half-reasonable to look at.

Which doesn't mean matching fluorescent green suits, ruffled pink shirts and colour-co-ordinated yellow bow ties. Unless you really, really want to. Good luck with that kids' TV show.

'Matching' outfits, unless you're a show band, is usually not a terribly good idea. If the entire band is wearing something that is quietly similar, however, that's a very good thing; it'll tie you together as a band without looking like a uniform.

The 'band look' is something that demands a lengthy discussion, plenty of suggestions and a general agreement. Find a style that you're all happy to wear, from the shy introvert to the daring or unembarrassable glam freak. Set a direction and some vague limits, then work out where within that you feel happiest. If you're going for a roughly formal look, that can encompass anything from full suit and tie to dark jeans and an untucked shirt; just try to make sure that the greater the diversity of style, the greater the similarity of tone or colour, or vice versa.

But watch out for the maverick who strikes out on their own. One memorable example recently involved a veteran blues piano player and his band at a fairly prestigious London venue. The main man himself was in a dark suit, red shirt and a good hat; tidy and subtle, with the shirt bringing a little flash. His younger rhythm section (double bass, little jazz drum kit) had chimed in with similar dark trousers and shirts, one with a red kerchief to match the boss's colour choice.

YOU WEAR IT WELL

Very smart. Then there was the guitarist. He wore a blue, yellow, pink and brown Hawaiian shirt and played a bright orange rock guitar. Effect entirely ruined. I do hope he was sacked shortly after that gig. Or at least locked up by the Fashion Police for a very long time.

As we're mostly aiming for a reasonably dignified elder statesman look rather than lurid teen popster, going a little conservative is a fine thing (small c, Clash fans).

Darker colours are a good start. There is a well-known idea that dark tones, and particularly black, are more slimming. This is not necessarily true; a skin-tight black T-shirt stretched over an impressive paunch is not really making much difference at all. But it does have the effect of your silhouette appearing a little more vague; a good thing for those of us whose silhouette is already a little, shall we say, ill-defined. Also, wearing much the same tones from top to bottom helps blur that tricky mid-section quite nicely. Conversely, wearing, say, dark jeans and a white T-shirt calls attention to the join between the two bits – which is fine if you're stick-thin but a lot less flattering if, like most of us, you've filled out a little bit recently.

That midriff area is the cause of a lot of grief for those of us with a generous amount of padding. Another trick to divert attention away is to visually shift your waistline – stop wearing those Top Gun-style bomber jackets and tight jeans, and go for a longer style of jacket or shirt. Not so long that you look like you've turned up in your nightshirt or joined the Teddy boys, but a good few inches below the waistline, with a more generous cut that doesn't hug those curves quite so tightly.

Long-sleeved tops are a good thing too; they add a little sobriety to the standard T-shirt. Unless they've got a comedy slogan on the front, of course, which is another no-no. If you really must wear something with writing or a logo on the front, keep it simple, graphic and classic. Old British motorcycle makes, or the Ace Cafe logo, are good standbys for rock 'n' rollers; a monochrome portrait of a legendary hero can work, provided it's vaguely relevant (your favourite Che Guevara shirt might not go down well at your Conservative Club gig); but nobody's going to be terribly impressed with your multicoloured, peeling Lanzarote souvenir shirt.

And then there's footwear. If you're playing a type of music that demands a certain type of shoe (cowboy boots, Dr Martens, suede brothel creepers...) then go for it. Otherwise stay neutral and muted. Bright white trainers? Ugh. Shiny grey patent leather moccasins? Oh dear. Sandals and socks? Instant, painful death.

You will find, however, that shoes influence the way you move around on stage. Lighter shoes will make you feel more mobile, big boots will root you solidly to the spot. Horses for courses – but again try to make sure the band are roughly in sync with their footwear choices. Having four people in scuffed sneakers and one in glittery platform boots will be a little odd.

But whatever you decide on as your 'band look', try to have a little fun with it. You might be the most boring dresser in an office full of grey-suited drones during the week, but it's a chance to indulge your inner extrovert a little.

And people may well have paid good money to watch

you strut your stuff. Pay them back by making a little effort. Isn't it worth investing in a decent shirt? Go on – you won't turn into Liberace. Probably.

GOOD... AND NOT SO GOOD

For a very brief period, Slade were one of the coolest bands in the world. Slade? Yes, Slade – the Black Country clowns best known for a huge and inescapable Christmas hit and frankly appalling dress sense.

Their career, apart from a brief false start as a skinhead band complete with bovver boots and Harrington jackets, was mostly marked by a total absence of taste. Dave Hill, the guitarist, had a frankly odd pudding-bowl haircut, enormous knee-high glitter platform boots and played a guitar shaped like a penis and emblazoned with the words 'Super Yob'. Bass and violin player Jim Lea rocked a pair of skintight court jester-style chequered leggings. Singer Noddy Holder was best known for a mirror-encrusted top hat, enormously flared, checked suits and such terrifyingly huge sideburns that looked like someone had glued a small dog to each side of his face.

And yet, briefly, they were cool. How? The story goes like this. In 1980, the Reading Festival was in deep trouble. One of their headline acts, Ozzy Osbourne, had cancelled at very short notice. Possibly he'd eaten a dodgy bat.

Reading in those days was a far cry from the slick, teen-friendly pop festival it is now. It was the grubbiest of all the festivals, mostly populated by the hardest of hard rock fans, a charming bunch who were renowned for their poor personal hygiene, their vast intake of alcohol and cheap drugs, and their impressive aim with a cider bottle full of urine. If they took even a mild dislike to a band, a hail of projectiles would take flight like an artillery barrage and force the hapless musicians off stage.

So when Ozzy dropped out and the only band who were available turned out to be comedy pop-rockers Slade, whose last major hits had been five years before, and who were on the verge of breaking up, it seems there was only one possible ending, which involved a mirrored top hat exploding into a million pieces under a sustained can and bottle assault.

But once Slade had talked their tour-weary guitarist into rejoining for what he was told was their farewell gig, they got on stage and triumphed. Far from falling on their faces in front of rock's toughest crowd, they won them over and tore the metaphorical roof off the place.

What most Brits hadn't realised was that far from disappearing off the face of the Earth, Slade had been slogging their way across America with big-name acts such as Aerosmith, Black Sabbath and ZZ Top, honing their stagecraft and working on winning over sceptical and disinterested foreign audiences.

The crowd of leathery rockers were duly converted, and Slade became a sudden, surprise success in the world of proper rock. They were booked for the equally hard-rocking Monsters of Rock festival and duly blew several tight-trousered rock titans clean off the stage.

Which posed a bit of a dilemma when it came to their image. Comedy trousers, amusing haircuts and silly hats were a little out of step with the heavy metal fashions of the day, which were tottering gradually towards theatrical, spandex-trousered excess.

Also, even then Slade weren't the youngest band on the block. They formed in 1966, for goodness' sake, and it wasn't even most of the members' first bands. The make-up and lycra leggings probably weren't an option. So what to do?

Someone had a stroke of genius. And next time the foursome walked on stage to serenade the metalheads, they'd changed their image completely.

They'd obviously been watching a few westerns – their new look involved floor-scraping duster coats, shitkicking boots, Mexican silver belts, stetsons, a dash of leather and lots and lots of black. And somehow it worked. They looked like a tough-as-old-boots cross between a border biker gang and the last desperados in town. Suddenly, the old Midlands comedians were cool and ever so slightly menacing.

It was a brief and brilliant comeback; they returned to the USA with their new image and new-found rock credentials, and had a few years of relative success and surprising influence (half of America's huge rock bands claim to have been big Slade fans).

It wasn't to last, sadly; they reverted back to their previous comedy pop clobber, went into the business of nostalgia and revival circuit retreads, then broke up, re-formed, broke up again, began again with only a few original members, and so on.

But for one glorious moment the most unlikely band in the world became really, really cool. There's a lesson in there somewhere for all of us.

But they're not the only veterans to take a few tips

from. All the greats have got a few sartorial tricks up their well-tailored sleeves (although in some cases it's more a dire warning than a recommendation).

Consider, for instance, at the two best-known and arguably most influential pop/rock bands in the world, The Beatles and The Stones. Looked at as bands, they both had distinctive images that changed with the times. But view them as a bunch of individuals and you can pick out who's got the visual staying power and who hasn't.

In The Beatles, it was more difficult to pick out individual differences thanks to their habit of dressing in matching costumes, both early on with suits and during their mid-period psychedelic pomp. But when they didn't dress alike, you could spot who had it and who didn't. Ringo always went a bit comedy, Paul was a bit unadventurous, John was all over the place (particularly post-Beatles with white suits, ethnic robes, army fatigues and, on one memorable occasion, nothing at all) – but George was always the one who had enough flair to be interesting without being wacky as they left their co-ordinated period. A white shirt, a bit of well-worn denim, maybe a well-cut jacket; rarely anything too flashy or silly. And, importantly, his taste still looked good as he aged – that English understatement served him well all the way through his career.

With The Stones, though, as their career has progressed their dress sense, in some cases, hasn't. Mick Jagger's outfit at their recent massive arena gigs, with its glam-rock barrow-boy look complete with trilby, wouldn't have looked out of place in the

YOU WEAR IT WELL

1970s. Keith Richards' piratical pose is now looking a little bit odd on a bloke who's more greybeard than Bluebeard. Ronnie Wood, as ever, just does what Keith does with the volume turned down a bit. But do you know who's the coolest of them all? The drummer. Yes, Charlie Watts, whose love of cool jazz and sense of when not to make a noise has served him so well all these years, still looks very sharp indeed in nicely cut suits, well-fitting, understated polo shirts and an air of detached amusement.

The jazz greats he idolises, of course, were big fans of the sharp suit, as were and are many of the blues greats. B.B. King, Muddy Waters and John Lee Hooker all felt that when you were going on stage you had to look that little bit sharper, cooler and more impressive than your audience. As B.B. King is reputed to be the father of around 15 illegitimate children, his look was clearly also a big hit with the ladies.

The lesson from all of those is that as you get on a bit, it's always worth dialling down the volume somewhat and turning up the sophistication. It never hurts to be a little more formal and tidier as you mature. It looks dignified rather than dull when you're a musician. By all means liven it up and loosen it up a bit (you don't really want to look like an undertaker or a chartered accountant) but start with some classic basics.

There are exceptions, of course. Neil Young is still rocking some variation of the ragged Navajo/hippy/farmhand thing that he's been doing for ever. Does he look cool? Not really. Does he care? Not at all. And let's face it, he's flipping Neil Young. He could wear a flowery poncho and still be a legend. Unless you're him, or a close associate, you can't get away with that sort of behaviour.

No, neat and slightly understated is the look to aim for – and that goes for hair too. As someone who may be follicly challenged, and is certainly unlikely to have a mane of glossy, bouffant hair, try to keep the instances of bald on top/long at the sides to a minimum. We've all seen the great comb-over disasters of the '70s, with Arthur Scargill and Bobby Charlton sporting wayward strands scraped loosely across from ear to ear. Don't go there. Short and tidy is fine.

Beards, though, are tempting. But while a full beard on a younger musician can make you look like a member of an Oregon psychedelic folk band, on an older person it's more likely to evoke village idiots, loony hermits, Rasputin or Cap'n Birdseye. Unless you're in ZZ Top, of course.

Lesser face furniture is remarkably popular – goatees, particularly, are often used in an attempt to summon up some jazz vibes. If you've got a long, thin face and/ or a prominent conk, this can work pretty well. If you've got a wide, flat or round face, though, they can look like a ring of navel fluff round a bathtub plughole. Think carefully.

Still, any minor facial hair like this is only a swipe of a razor away from being erased or converted into something else. Don't be afraid to experiment; you might come up with something that suits you perfectly. Try anything and everything. Somewhere in the spectrum from Frank Zappa's carefully manicured 'tache and soul patch arrangement to Seasick Steve's wild straggle of chin fur might be your perfect facial adornment.

But back to the head, and the vexed question of hats. It's always a reasonable workaround if you've reached the sort of age where the shine from the top of your head is blinding people in the first three rows. But which?

If you're in the sort of outfit that welcomes hats, from stetsons to berets, trilbies to rasta caps, your choice is easy. Get the right sort of hat, make sure it fits well enough not to fall on the floor the first time you nod your head but doesn't cut off the blood supply to your ears, and you're good to go.

If you're not genre-bound, though, headwear can be tricky. Again, the first rule is understatement. A rebel flag biker bandana may have worked for Axl Rose, but you're not him. A purple glitter stetson may have its place, but that place is atop a 19-year-old clubber in Ibiza, not distracting everybody who's trying to listen to your music.

Try starting off with something darkish, unflashy and relatively sober. And try to find a hat that suits the shape of your face. Guitar legend Richard Thompson is rarely seen without a beret, but then he has the sort of pointed, thin face that makes it look rather good. A beret-wearer with a fatter visage would resemble an overcooked Yorkshire pudding. So try something with a taller crown if you're rotund of features.

Once you start looking, you realise how wide your options are. John Lee Hooker had a very fine semi-trilby type of arrangement. Tom Waits often wears a bowler hat (but then he's Tom Waits so can get away with almost anything). David Crosby's Byrds-era hat was a rather good flat-topped Borsalino. There are plenty more. Just take look at your favourite album covers.

Trucker caps are a little bit of a cliché these days (unless paired with faded dungarees and a country/blues howl, in which case it's rather a good cliché). And baseball caps are distinctly iffy, though your classic hip-hop outfit channelling Run DMC would no doubt disagree.

But if in doubt just give it a try. Remember, you're on stage to entertain, so provided you don't look utterly ridiculous a little bit of restrained showmanship is a good thing. Learn where the line is between mildly extrovert and frankly stupid and try not to fall over the edge of it too often.

Look and listen to your bandmates; do you look like a coherent band, or a collection of strangers who don't share any common clothing tastes? Do your onstage outfits look casually considered, or do you appear to have just wandered in from mowing the lawn? Do they complement your music, distract from it, or clash horribly with what you're trying to achieve?

No, dressing up is not really the point of what you do. It's not a vital part of your sound, and it's not going to make any difference to your talent or competence (though some claim that being dressed better makes you play better).

But it should make you appear like you mean it, and stop you looking an idiot. That's important. It's worth spending a few minutes thinking about it. You won't turn into Elton John, honest. Though if dressing up can make a plump, balding, nearsighted bloke from Watford called Reg into a worldwide superstar, it's certainly worth a bit of your time.

STAGE MOVES

Shake your hips, the Rolling Stones recommended. Also, you can shake your moneymaker (Elmore James), shake your booty (KC & the Sunshine Band) or do the hippy hippy shake (The Swinging Blue Jeans). That's a whole lot of shaking (Jerry Lee Lewis).

Do you have to? No. Should you? Quite possibly. As you get a little more creaky and self-conscious, it's always an easy option to stand stock still and hope that the music speaks for itself. This can work if you're playing something fiercely complicated and intellectual, where the merest twitch of a leg would be frowned upon. You didn't see prog-rock bands do a lot of shimmying, let's face it. And John Coltrane was never known as much of a go-go dancer.

But if you're playing music that's aimed at the pelvis as well as the cortex, it makes sense that you look like you're enjoying it too. If you're inciting people to put on their dancing shoes and boogie, it doesn't make much sense for you to look aloof and disapproving like an old, grumpy janitor on disciplinary duty at the school disco.

So where's the line between enthusiastic and undignified? That's a tricky one. The difference is probably whether it looks natural or forced. Are you grooving along to your music and therefore moving about a bit, or are you forcing yourself into a series of semi-rehearsed routines? The former is engaging, the latter can be embarrassing unless you're very good.

If it's actually a well-rehearsed, slick, dance routine, though, well done. It worked for The Shadows, The Stylistics (plus many other great soul bands) and Madonna. There's no reason it won't wow them at the Dribblesworth & District Women's Institute Hall. Er, maybe.

Of course not everybody can dance. In two different ways. In a purely literal way, not every member of the band can actually get up and boogie. Drummers are pretty much stuck. Keyboard players are usually rooted to the spot, unless you're playing one of those shocking '80s Keytar things that look like a mutant offspring of a synthesiser and a guitar. In which case you shouldn't be rooted to the spot; you should be nailed to a tree instead.

Guitarists and bass players do have the option to at least move about a bit – though double bass players are a bit more encumbered – and really should. No, you don't want to bump into each other or crash through the drum kit, but just stepping forward when you take a solo or moving into the mike to share backing vocals at least gives some sense of activity. Standing still, staring down at your effects pedals and scowling may have been briefly popular for the aptly named shoegaze bands, but it's not terribly friendly.

And singers have no excuse. If you've got nothing to get in your way but the occasional bit of harmonica, maracas or tambourine, then you should take the opportunity to liven things up a bit. If it's a small stage, at least try to move from side to side a little; stroll about, change your position, make eye contact with different areas of the audience. And try to move to the rhythmic parts. Nobody's expecting Michael Jackson-style dance pyrotechnics, but the occasional mild shimmy or twitch of a leg isn't too much to hope for.

Then there's the other sort of people who can't dance

– the ones who, however hard they try, can't seem to get their body in sync with the beat. Or possibly have an embarrassing, flailing sort of uncoordinated flapping dad-dance style. This is bad, but it's not terminal. At least use your arms – point, clap, gesticulate. Walk about a bit. Don't use your lack of choreographic talent as a reason to wimp out of your responsibility to get your audience moving.

You're never too old to rock 'n' roll, to paraphrase Jethro Tull. Whose frontman made them famous by standing on one leg, pulling faces and playing the flute. You see, it doesn't really matter what you do, provided you do it convincingly.

CHAPTER 9

KEEP ON RUNNING

This is the bargain bin of the book – the stuff that wouldn't quite fit neatly into the rest of the sections. Like any record shop bargain bin, there will hopefully be the occasional gem hidden between a Brotherhood of Man album and six copies of that Fleetwood Mac record that nobody can ever remember the name of but everybody owned for about three weeks in 1987.

If you've made it this far, you've probably noticed that there's been very little about eardrums, vans and felt-tip pens. You're in luck – this is where that sort of thing lives.

You'll also have observed that there's been precious little effort to provide exhaustive lists of recommended gear, upcoming gigs and current trends in musical technology. That's because this stuff changes on an almost minute-by-minute basis. Purely in the gap between this book being written and it appearing in the shops, about half the things you'll want to know will have changed, making you feel a bit disgruntled and us feel like idiots. By the time this book's been out a couple of years, all that stuff would look like a historical document. When was the last time you looked in the Magna Carta to find out somebody's postcode?

However, there's a set of useful sources of up-to-date information in the next chapter. While it's tricky (well, actually impossible) to do real-time updating of a printed book, we'll try to point you in the direction of some people who make it their business to keep up with all that stuff.

That said, while they have high technology on their side it's still awkward to read a website in the bath. We're definitely ahead on that one.

So here's a big bargain bin of randomness for your delectation. There's bound be something in here to your taste; it'll probably be hidden behind a German synth-prog band's third album, though. Good luck.

VOLUME AND DEAFNESS

Are you, by any chance, starting to have a few issues with your hearing? I SAID, ARE YOU...

All right, it's a cheap joke. And if you've been playing, or even just listening to, loud music for a long time it's not even that funny. Because it's probably true.

It's a fact that as you get older, your hearing tends to deteriorate. It happens at different rates in different people, and may take several different forms, but there's no way of getting round that reality. And if you've abused your eardrums for years, it's likely to happen sooner and get worse faster. This is bad.

However, there are quite a few things you can do – both to prevent it getting any worse and to help deal with it when it's already a bit cronky.

The first thing you can do is blindingly obvious, but not always popular – turn down a bit. Or a lot. If you're in a loud band, make it clear to everybody that you're not happy with the volume level, explain that you're worried about your hearing and make it plain that you're entirely serious about this.

This will have one of two possible results. Either your fellow musicians will apologise and immediately start exploring ways of playing more quietly, or they won't. Your choices then are to continue and risk lasting damage (bad) or to leave and find some other players who are more civilised (not great, but better than option A).

This sort of thing can divide bands; you'll often find that one or more will fervently agree, while others will disagree equally violently. There is, after all, a certain excitement in playing loudly; it adds energy and makes you feel as though you really mean it.

The person who's most likely to object to reduced volume is, of course, the drummer. Their instrument is for the most part acoustic and they feel, possibly rightly, that it sounds best when thumped extremely hard. This makes a great deal of racket.

They do have a point: a big drum kit being given a walloping by somebody both physical and skilled is a rare treat and adds a propulsive energy like a speeding freight train to any song. And the physical exertion is, for many drummers, part of the package. That's why they enjoy it. The thought of merely tickling a tiny kit with knitting needle-thin sticks or brushes turns them right off.

Guitarists, too, can be unashamedly loud. Once seduced by the power of a big, loud valve amp set to 11, it's difficult to go back to weedy little combos. The mighty roar of the classic rock guitar noise (Les Paul through Marshall, usually) is again a great thing, and very tricky to reproduce accurately at lower volume levels; the sound level is part of the effect.

These are fine sounds. But are they worth swapping for your ability to hear birdsong, conversation or your mobile? That's what it could come down to. Hearing damage, in its simplest form, usually hits your higher frequencies first. It often happens anyway as we age, but prolonged exposure to high noise levels speeds up the process. The net result is like putting a blanket over your ears; it muffles and smothers the sounds we hear.

Of course, one of the major things we listen to is human conversation, and this sort of damage makes life particularly irritating; it knocks out our abilities to pick out the high-pitched, short consonant sounds in speech like 's' and 't'. It doesn't mean we can't hear talking, but it makes it far more difficult to pick out the gist of what's being said, especially in a crowded or noisy space. You'll start finding that a one-to-one conversation somewhere relatively quiet is fine, but in a busy pub you'll strain to catch what somebody else is saying. It sounds like they're mumbling. They're not, but your ears are not catching the top end, which is the bit that makes speech intelligible.

This is, usually, non-reversible; it's a one-way trip to the world of hearing aids and asking people to speak up. Though an ear trumpet would be a rather fetching fashion accessory. There are probably some hipsters in Shoreditch using them right now. Ironically, of course.

If you're starting to get that sort of problem, go and see your doctor. Don't wait. It won't go away. Try to get referred to a specialist and get a proper test done, so you know what the damage is so far, and take their advice on what to do next. One bit of which is likely to be "Stop playing in noisy bands." Oh. Back to that again.

Somewhere in that visit to the GP you may be advised to get your ears syringed, micro-suctioned or otherwise given a good hoovering. This may help – it'll make your hearing feel squeaky-clean – but it doesn't tend to last all that long, so don't be fooled by a sudden drastic improvement and go back to blasting away at 300 watts again. High volume can actually be more damaging when your protective layer of earwax has been disposed of, so be particularly careful.

The other sort of hearing damage, one which is more mysterious but in some ways far more annoying, is tinnitus. This usually takes the form of whistling or whining noises that can be heard when there are no other external sounds. It sounds like a dodgy neon light or your fridge on the blink, but it's actually your own ears, or the bit of brain that works them, malfunctioning. This is often linked to long exposure to high levels of volume, and musicians are especially prone to it (even Beethoven complained about tinnitus. He should have turned those amps down a bit).

There are various therapies being trialled, but nobody quite knows what the underlying physical cause of tinnitus is. One thing we do know, however, is that it's spectacularly irritating, and can badly disrupt sleep in severe cases – it's been linked to at least one suicide case.

But as with most things, the best way to deal with it is not to get it in the first place. Turn those amps down. Don't rehearse at high volume. And have a word with the drummer. A really loud word.

KEEP ON RUNNING

LIVE ISSUES

If you're gigging regularly, you'll have got yourself pretty much sorted. Your gear is portable and reliable. You carry around plenty of spares in case things go wrong. You can get yourselves set up quickly and efficiently. You're slick on stage and well drilled when it comes to loading in, loading out and packing up.

But there's always the random factor. And not many factors are as random as the stuff you'll come across when you're out playing. Some of these will not so much put a spanner in the works as a whole toolkit.

The first is other bands or artists. If you're on a bill with more than one act, you'll have to deal with the politics that inevitably come into play.

The first item on the agenda, of course, is who plays when. Conventional wisdom has it that the act with the biggest audience plays last and gets their name at the top of the posters – hence the term headlining. But sometimes it's not easy to tell who's the biggest draw. And sometimes last is not necessarily where you want to play. That's where it gets a bit complicated.

If a promoter's running the show, they'll make the decision. It may not be a decision you agree with, but as the first time you find out about it is usually when the posters are already printed and the ads have gone out, hard cheese. It's their show; you can whinge if you like but it's their call.

If you really think that you're the big star(s) and deserve your name much larger than anybody else's, the time to discuss this is when you first book, or confirm, the gig. Not later when it's all done and dusted.

But you'd better back up your groovier-than-thou

attitude with solid statistics. Can you really bring many more people than the other acts? Will you sell many more CDs, T-shirts or other bits of merchandising? Will your name get the gig featured on the radio or in the press? If so, good. Headliner status awaits. If not, you'll look a bit stupid when everybody turns up to see the support acts then trails off into the night, or the other bar, when you come on.

In fact, that often happens at multi-band gigs; fans will turn up to see their own favourite, then ignore the rest. Some venues are worse than others for this. If there's just one big room, and everybody's in for the duration it's fine. If there's a second bar or annexe people can escape to, they often will. And if there are hefty soundproof doors between the main gig room and the bar, as often happens these days in venues with noise issues and nearby neighbours, that's worse. Not only will people hide in the bar, but they often won't even be able to tell when you go on stage. Being ignored by other acts' fans isn't great, but being missed by your own is downright annoying.

And one other feature of those multiple gigs is that when people turn up to see a particular act, they'll turn up fairly early but leave straight after their favourites have played. In which case, if you want the maximum crowd you need to be on mid-evening, as by the end only your own fans will still be there, plus a few insomniacs and drunks. It's worth remembering this before somebody throws a tantrum about going on last – it might not always be the perfect spot.

If you have to sort this out between yourselves, and there's not a clear headline act, there's a simple rule –

the act who did the most work should get the choice of when to play. If you've just breezed along that night while another act has been leafleting the town and marketing the gig online like mad, it's only fair to let them have the rewards of their labours.

But sometimes fairness and courtesy go out of the window and it comes down to who got there first and who's got the sharpest elbows and the loudest voice. But think – is it really that important? You're not playing Wembley Arena (if you are, however, hello Broooooce). If you're anywhere local, it's highly likely that you'll end up playing with some of these acts again. Be diplomatic and use your common sense. Don't get all egotistical and wind everybody up.

And if somebody else is doing just that, then let them have their petty tantrum. It'll be crystal clear to all concerned that they're being a bit of a prat. Be grown-up and make it plain that you're doing them a bit of a favour, out of the kindness of your heart, and that next time they owe you one.

If they're total gits, of course (and there are certainly a few in the world of music), this won't work. Neither, unfortunately, will socking them in the nose with a cymbal stand. Which is certainly what you'll feel like doing. Take a step back, take a deep breath and hold your temper. If there's a promoter or a landlord involved, have a quiet word later on; mention that you've stepped aside for the sake of a smooth-running show, but also indicate that you'd like to be considered for the top spot next time round (ideally on a bill without those gits involved).

So now you've got the running order sorted out, you

have to deal with the other thorny multi-act gig issue: gear. Transport is a hassle for most musicians, but not every venue has its own in-house equipment, and if they do then it's most likely to be pretty well abused and of a deeply dubious standard. So the solution is often to see if some sort of gear sharing can be arranged.

This can be a giant can of very wriggly worms. The big, not-easily-portable bits are usually things like bass amps and drum kits. Guitarists may well be picky about their amps, keyboard players will usually bring their own familiar keyboard, and most other musicians need little more than can be carried on public transport.

Bass amps are relatively straightforward: if they work and are loud enough, clear enough and not unmanageably complex they'll do the job. In some cases the bass can even be plugged directly into the PA, via a DI box – bassists may want to invest in a decent one of these if they're going ampless often. Easy.

Drum kits, however, are complicated bits of musical Meccano that have to stand up to being hit hard and repeatedly. They can break in all sorts of ways, many messy and expensive, and every drummer has his or her particular way of setting one up. However, a good rule when sharing is always that each drummer brings their own 'breakables' – usually cymbals, snare and bass drum pedal. At least that's most of the likely damage candidates taken care of.

The golden rule is always to get this worked out well in advance and make sure it's confirmed by all concerned. Turning up to a faraway gig with two bass amps but no drum kit would be highly embarrassing. Make sure everybody's happy about the arrangement, too, so deal directly with the owner of the gear if possible, rather than another member. "Of course so-and-so will be happy to lend their priceless amp" might turn into "No, I never lend my amp to anybody" at short notice unless you get it from the horse's mouth.

Of course, there are examples of less organised sharing – often when something's gone wrong. It's hardly unusual for a worried-looking guitarist, for instance, to sprint over and ask to borrow an amp because theirs has gone on the blink. This is usually fine. And if they're unable to play otherwise, it seems mean to refuse. But make sure you help them set it up, talk them through the settings and the switches, and keep a wary eye open. And warn them to be careful with it. Has their amp broken randomly, or because they're a clumsy berk who keeps tipping them over, smashing their guitar into the front or turning them up until the innards glow red hot? Whoops, crash, there goes yours too. Oh dear.

What happens if another band breaks your gear is another potential can of worms. Naturally, all musicians are honest and pleasant people who will immediately offer to pay for any repairs and offer sincere apologies. Aren't they? Er, no.

Remember to check your stuff after someone else has been using it. Don't just load it into the car or van and ignore it until the next rehearsal – give it a quick look over. Has anyone spilled a beer into the back? Has it suddenly acquired a dent or major scratch? Does it still have all its leads, knobs, feet and so on?

If your gear's been trashed, have a word immediately. Be polite, but be firm. Point out the damage (they may not have noticed it themselves) and if possible explain what it'll take to get fixed. If you've dug them out of a hole, they'd have to be a special kind of bastard not to be sympathetic. If they really don't appear to give a flying one, try not to give in to your understandable urge to belt them, particularly if the adrenalin's running high after a gig. Are they the bandleader? If not, find out who is and go and talk to them instead. Tell the promoter or landlord. If they think an act is being antisocial, they may well think twice about booking them again. The idea of losing a few gigs might make paying for a small repair or two seem like a relative bargain.

But don't get greedy. If someone's dented your bass drum head that doesn't mean they owe you a whole new kit. Be reasonable and realistic. And bear in mind that it's live music gear, and therefore should be built to stand up to a certain amount of punishment. You're not talking about a crystal chandelier, unless you're Liberace of course, you're speaking about a big heavy object, usually made of wood.

If you're really twitchy, or you have something very rare, valuable and irreplaceable, you can always say no. In which case, prepare to be treated as a churlish idiot. And also ask yourself why you're taking something like that to a gig, where major damage is always only one clumsy musician, distracted engineer or drunken fan away.

Gear is also the subject of one other random factor, and a bit of a dirty little secret – theft. Always, always keep a careful eye on your stuff. Some acts have light-fingered members, some fans have a nasty habit of subsidising their gig tickets with a bit of pilfering, and it's not unknown for staff at venues to have a sneaky swipe or two if they think no one's looking.

Musical gear is often extremely portable and of relatively high value. Something like an effects pedal or a microphone can vanish in seconds. Guitars in cases are an obvious target; stealing guitars out of cases but leaving the case is a devious way of covering tracks for a few vital minutes. Then there's all the minor stuff – leads, sticks, small bits of percussion, tools, tuners and so on.

If you suspect another band of lifting something in that category, don't immediately come over all Poirot and accuse all and sundry; it's quite likely to be an honest mistake. One lead looks much the same as another in the heat of post-gig packing up. Mention it without being rude. "You haven't seen something that looks like this, have you?"

And mark all your kit. A ring of coloured insulating tape round the plugs works to pick leads out as yours and avoids arguments. You don't have to stencil the band name all over your amps and cases (though it does look a bit flash) but use some sort of ID, even if it's just felt-tip pen initials on the inside of a drum head or a small sticker somewhere unobtrusive on a cymbal, guitar or keyboard.

If you're one of those players who scatters effects pedals loosely all over the stage, don't. Get a pedal board and stick everything securely to it. Firstly it'll be more reliable and take much less setting up; secondly, it'll make it more difficult for the light-fingered to liberate your pedals.

But the golden rule is never to leave anything unattended. Don't place a big pile of gear in the dressing room or backstage corridor and all go for a curry. If you have to deposit stuff in a car, put it in the boot out of sight or at least cover it up. Be safe out there. Evening all.

TRANSPORT, ROADIES ETC

You only ever play in central London, and you're in an all-acoustic band featuring mandolin, ukelele, harmonica and bongos. You rehearse at home and can get to all of your gigs on the bus, train or tube. You could probably cycle at a pinch. Well done. You have no need to read this.

But for the rest of us, transport is a bit of an issue. For although music is the product of a voice and a few instruments, it seems to demand a vast amount of large, heavy equipment. And both rehearsal and gig venues have a terrible habit of being rather inaccessible. From the rehearsal rooms on the industrial estate by the gas works to the lovely but remote country pub, some form of motorised transport always seems to be a necessary evil.

A truly organised band will, of course, have a van and a roadie. This seems like a luxury, and in some cases it is. But it's rather a good one. If you could, why wouldn't you? Even if you're not remotely professional, the idea of getting your gear and possibly yourself delivered at a convenient time, then having an expert at hand to load in and set up your gear – plus the reverse at the end of the night when you're knackered – sounds blissful.

It needn't even be terribly expensive. If you're not in London, there are plenty of cheap vans around at the moment thanks to the capital's Low Emissions Zone, which has banned many older vehicles from inside the M25 and meant that quite a few otherwise usable, if antiquated, vans have been sold off cheap out of town. Have a whip-round; for the price of a couple of decent lunches each you might find that you could pick up a reasonable runner. Add up the amount of fuel you're using if you all drive to gigs with your gear separately, and you may find it makes financial sense.

The roadie is a little trickier to get cheap, if you're after somebody experienced and professional. But you probably don't need a big bloke in a Hawkwind tour jacket with a mammoth bunch of keys on his belt and a ponytail. Surely you must know somebody who could be persuaded to give you a hand with driving and lifting in exchange for a bit of pocket money and the odd free beer?

It's not as unattractive an offer as you might think. To outsiders, the world of music still seems glamorous and cool. They will, of course, soon find out that there's nothing remotely glamorous about hauling a speaker cabinet up four flights of stairs or driving 120 miles in a rainstorm to find the venue's closed down, but by that time you've already got them involved. Your evil plan has worked. Mwahaha and so on.

So have you got a friend, a sibling or even a willing workmate who'd give a hand? Once they've agreed, you're at liberty to train them in the dark arts of setting up gear, bolting together drum kits and tuning guitars and turn them into a genuinely useful extra member.

There are a few potential problems with this arrangement, however. Firstly, you have to trust your recruit's driving skills, navigational talents, organisational sense and self-control when free beer is on offer. A lost, pissed, dangerous roadie with no working mobile is not much of an asset.

Secondly, you need to think about security. Do you leave your gear in the van overnight, or even for long stretches of time? Unless it's parked somewhere seriously secure, that's not a great idea. Which means unloading it somewhere, usually very, very late at night. This is boring and inconvenient, but better than losing all your expensive kit. A reasonable halfway house is to take the expensive bits out, but leave large, relatively difficult-to-nick items like speaker cabs and stands in the van. But even then you have to make sure your locks and alarms are up to scratch. Just assume that an unattended van will be broken into sooner rather than later and take any steps necessary to minimise the damage. Keeping a big angry dog inside is certainly an amusing option, but it's quite tricky to clean Rottweiler dribble off drum cases.

But if the van seems a little too much cash, hassle or pretension for you there's no reason why you couldn't still enlist a roadie to help out. If it makes them feel better you can always call them a 'stage technician', of course, but basically anybody who's happy with doing a good chunk of the heavy lifting and helping to plug things in correctly is worth their weight in gold. Or at least pork scratchings. If they're also willing to take on tasks like mending knackered cables, selling tickets on the door or tuning guitars for mid-set replacement, they're even more valuable than that. Scampi Fries, possibly.

All arriving in separate vehicles to every gig doesn't make a lot of sense, unless like The Eagles or Pink Floyd you are continually tangled up in a pile of lawsuits and hate each other's guts; you really ought to work out a basic rota of who drives and who picks up who. If you all live miles apart this may not work, but for everybody else it's simply sensible. It'll save fuel, mean that navigation can also be shared, and also that at least a few of the band can have a beer after the gig without worrying about drink-driving. Organise it well beforehand, so everybody knows what's going on.

And don't be late. If you're supposed to be picking somebody up at 7.15, don't suddenly realise that you need petrol, double back to pick up your satnav/phone/ guitar, stop in a layby to have a sandwich and arrive at 8.20.

Gigs are no fun at all when you're already stressed and rushed by the time you arrive. Leave plenty of time and if you're going to be unavoidably late ensure that people know about it so they can make excuses, cover for you, or let another act do their soundcheck first.

Don't forget security when you have your gear in a car too. Don't leave it in sight. Your car may have a super-duper high-security alarm system, but all it takes is a villain with half a brick – they'll be well away with your beloved instrument before everybody figures out what that strange warbling noise is.

And if you're all loading your equipment into various vehicles after the gig, be organised. Keep one person on duty outside to look after everybody's gear. Many a bit of kit has gone missing from a pub car park, while distraught musicians say "I thought you were looking after it." "No, I thought you were".

Also, finally, if you've got something even vaguely valuable, make sure it's properly insured. Not just for theft, but for accidental damage too. Check those pesky clauses on your home contents insurance or car policy and you may well find that there are limits on the value of individual items, exemptions for stuff left in a car overnight or other sneaky get-out provisos. Try getting some specialist instrument insurance, and if you do a lot of driving to and from gigs make absolutely sure that it covers you if some moron rear-ends you at a roundabout while your pride and joy is in the boot, or some other bit of automotive mayhem wrecks your gear.

It can even happen to the most famous musicians of all. In 1965 The Beatles were on tour, with all of their guitars strapped to the roof of the car. But some way up the M1 motorway, at full speed, the straps snapped and one fell off. It was George Harrison's beloved Gretsch Country Gentleman.

As he later recounted: "About thirteen lorries went over it before our chauffeur could get near it. Then, one of the lorries stopped and the driver came up with the dangling remains of it and said, 'Oi, is this banjo anything to do with you?'"

SET LISTS AND SO ON

Bits of paper are very useful things sometimes. Yes, of course we live in a digital, paperless, all-online world now. We're all fully wired, or wireless, or underwired, or something.

But when you're right in front of a bunch of people who are waiting for you to play the right songs, in the right key, at roughly the right tempo, in the right order, a piece of paper close at hand feels somehow... right.

The set list is one of the most vital things you can have on stage. It's both a cue sheet and a document of how you think the evening's going to go, what you think you're playing well and what effect you reckon your material will have at different stages of the gig.

In essence, they're simple. Write down all the songs you know how to play to a reasonable standard (keep this list – it's always handy to have a complete inventory of your material).

Then think about what sort of gig you're planning for. Mentally delete all the ones that don't fit – too quiet, too loud, too fast and so on – and cut the remainder down to a sensible length by taking out the weaker numbers.

There's your set list. All that remains to do is put it in the right order. The classic system is to kick off with a couple of good solid lively numbers to wake everyone up, stick some slower or more challenging ones towards the middle, then finish with some proven crowdpleasers, and maybe hold one or two aside for an encore if you're feeling confident. Job done.

This is assuming that you're playing a basic set of fairly populist material, of course. Your three-hour industrial jazz-metal total sonic assault gig may demand something more avant-garde, though, like playing all your songs in reverse alphabetical order or organising them by the number of times you play the note F sharp.

One entertaining alternative came from post-punk troubadour Elvis Costello, who played at least one tour with a giant roulette-style wheel in the middle of the stage featuring the titles of 40 songs. After each song he spun the wheel, then played whichever song the arrow pointed to next. Presumably there was an exemption for duplicates, otherwise a sticky axle could have caused a somewhat dreary evening of 'Watching the Detectives' 29 times.

You can also sneak other helpful information on to set lists; the key is often a good one if you've chopped and changed songs a few times. That's also useful when you're putting one together – too many songs in the same key will sound dull; too many huge jumps could sound bitty and confusing.

Tempo can be handy for drummers, and if you're using any gadgets that sync to the beat like tremolo or echo pedals you might need an exact beats per minute figure.

For those of us whose memory isn't quite what it used to be (all of us then), it's sometimes useful to have a note of who starts which song. It's always embarrassing to be waiting ages for someone to come in, then realise it's supposed to be you.

And talking of faculties that aren't totally top-notch, don't forget to write them out clearly and as large as possible. Printing gets you bonus marks, but just a decent thick felt-tip pen and some half-decent handwriting (capitals, please) should work perfectly well. Black on white is reliable – red, for instance, looks urgent and efficient in normal light but will often disappear completely once the stage lights kick in. Whoops.

KEEP ON RUNNING

Another advantage of doing them on a computer and printing them out, other than legibility, is that you have a permanent record of your set list from any given gig. It's too easy to leave your copies scattered all over the stage like rock 'n' roll confetti at the end of a night, then be unable to remember which particular combination of songs made everybody go crazy towards the end of your set (it might have been the cut-price cider, of course, but let's hope it was you). If you happen across a particularly good set, you can reprint it for the next venue and save yourself some hassle.

Also, doing them on a computer means you've written them in advance and may even have had a chance to email them round to other band members beforehand for comments and suggestions. This has the potential to turn into a major nuisance, with everybody changing their minds all the time and nobody agreeing on anything, so it needs one person to act as umpire. But at least it does allow some input from everyone, and nobody can say they weren't warned once they see the set list on the night.

Talking of which, many bands decide on and write out their set lists on the night itself, usually after the soundcheck. Assuming you've remembered the basics – plenty of paper and at least one working marker pen, preferably two – this can be a decent use of that dead time. If you're well-rehearsed and have a reliable, standard set it's perfectly OK. But if you're likely to squabble over it, do it well beforehand. You don't want to have a bitter scrap then all go on stage in various states of huff; it's no fun. It's also boring writing out set lists for a biggish band by hand, so it might be at least worth bringing a few more pens along and getting people to write their own.

And if you're the sort of people who get a bit lively on stage, or you're playing outdoors, you may want to tape them down. One gust of wind or ill-advised plimsoll swipe can leave you hopelessly adrift if your set list has wafted off to somewhere in row three.

And one final hint: if you're on a bill with another act or two, make sure it's actually your own set list that's taped down in front of you. There's been more than one occasion when what should be the beginning of the second song has turned into a frantic game of "I thought *you'd* brought them...".

STREAMLINING YOUR SET-UP

It's all too easy to end up with a rehearsal space that looks like a teenager's bedroom. Not necessarily including the cuddly toys and posters of appalling toothy popstars, but in the sense of being a random, overstuffed pile of things ranging from expensive and useful to pointless rubbish, arranged in no particular order and left in great heaps. "Oh mum," goes the whine when asked to tidy up, "but *I* know where everything is...".

Having the luxury of your own space, whether that's a proper studio, a spare room, a cellar or a shed, is a fine thing but it can lead to some bad habits when it comes to tidiness and order.

Of course, this might not be you. You may be the sort of neurotically organised individual who draws outlines round their tools on the garage wall and painstakingly indexes all their leads according to length, connector and colour.

Or, more likely, like most of us you're somewhere between the two. But one thing is certain – you've probably got too much stuff. You've definitely got too much stuff to take out with you when you're doing a gig or a proper offsite rehearsal.

Not that your stuff isn't all useful and valuable, but do you really need three broken guitar tuners, a six-inch lead with two banana plugs at one end and a five-pin DIN at the other, a shaker that has scattered all its dried peas over the floor and a cardboard box which once housed some long-sold bit of kit but has now been claimed by the cat?

No. You don't. But what litters your own personal music space is entirely up to you. It's not bothering anybody else (unless your anal-retentive keyboard player has to suppress a shudder every time it all arrives, of course) and it's not causing any impediment to your music making.

However, once you go elsewhere to play you'll need to transport and set up your stuff easily, quickly and without a great degree of faff. This is why you need to streamline your set-up.

The first step is to go extremely minimal. Think: what's the absolute least amount of gear you could manage with? No luxuries, no backups, no frills. One guitar, one lead, one amp? A stripped-down drum kit with no added percussion or flashy-looking but rarely used cymbals or toms? A single keyboard that will do most things tolerably well?

Now add a small bag of absolute essentials. A spare lead. A battery if your set-up involves anything non-mains-powered. Some paper and a pen if you're on set list duty or need some memory-jogging notes. Got a valve amp? Take a couple of spare valves, well protected (bubble wrap and tupperware is unglamorous but effective).

And a multi-tool, just in case. Swiss Army knives can be handy if they contain all the relevant bits; other people swear by Gerber or Leatherman. Or just a couple of screwdrivers and some pliers held together with a rubber band would work. Whatever you take, make sure it fits all the appropriate screws and nuts on whatever you're likely to be mending. If you're a drummer, you may well want to pack a spare drum key too. A small torch can be handy for peering round the back of things on dark stages.

If you play something electrical, you'll need at least one mains extension. For some reason most venues' mains plugs are located in the position of maximum inaccessibility, so being able to run power to where it's actually required is invaluable. Multi-socket extensions are ideal for flexibility, and if you use a powered pedal board you'll need to get power to the front of the stage as well as the back, so that's two extension leads.

And some gaffa tape as well. Also known as duct tape, duck tape, gaffer's tape, racer's tape, tank tape, rigger's tape and Alabama chrome, it's difficult to imagine life without this sticky essential. When not in use mending spacecraft, racing motorcycles or commandos' boots, it's a vital part of the live music industry. There can't be a stage in the country without the tell-tale gluey residue somewhere on it. From sticking down set lists to trip-proofing trailing leads, holding bits of drum stand together to forcing wobbly plugs to stay put, at some point you'll need gaffa tape.

So now you've got your absolute basics down, you'll want to expand that a bit and introduce some of your other bits of kit: the 'nice-to-haves' rather than the essentials. Don't forget that basic set-up, however; you could always get a last-minute gig, a car breakdown, a lift with someone short of space, or even a booking somewhere which necessitates flying.

As you add more items to bring you back to your ideal rehearsal set-up, consider each one closely. Do you really, really need it? Every piece of gear you drag along has to be loaded, unloaded, set up, plugged in or bolted together and tested, then the reverse at the end of the night. Every few minutes you add to the process means arriving that bit earlier and/or making everybody wait that bit longer.

Do you really need two amps for a stereo effect? Will the audience actually notice? Is it worth taking that extra keyboard for its superlative analogue synth sounds, when you only use it on one song and your main keyboard does a reasonably close imitation? Are you actually going to play those extra three toms? Does that fretless bass actually make a difference to the song, or just look flash?

Every time you add something, stop. Think. And remember that you're trying to entertain people; a process which is about keeping them interested and excited. Unless you're playing a music industry convention, your enormous array of expensive kit is unlikely to achieve that.

There's nothing wrong with a bit of gear fetishism – buying and playing decent instruments is one of life's great pleasures. But that double bass drum kit,

Hammond organ and wall of Marshall stacks become a lot less attractive when you have to haul them down a load of stairs at two in the morning.

Many musicians are actively trying to downsize their gear nowadays, and there are some great little amps about that make your previous lengthy load-in into a two-handed one-trip carry. Electronic drum kits sound remarkably realistic and pack up into a small box. Keyboard emulators now get at least 95% of the way to a good organ, piano or clavinet sound, even if they don't look quite as cool as half a ton of walnut and ivory.

And remember, the more you take, the more there is to go wrong. We've all spent some time cursing at a bit of gear that stubbornly refuses to work, when it was fine two days ago. However, the worst nightmare of all is the ultra-complex set-up, when just to find out what's gone wrong you have to dismantle something halfway between a 1950s telephone exchange and Cape Kennedy space centre. It could be one of the 235 leads, it could be a power connector, it could be a pedal or a junction box or a dodgy mains socket, or it could be just that the idiot's forgotten to turn the volume up on their instrument.

Try to think of that scenario before you decide to take everything you own along to a gig, and if you must go for a grandiose set-up, at least foolproof it a little bit by mounting things like pedals securely on boards, labelling or colour-coding particularly tricky cable runs, and having a plan B in case some wildly unreliable bit of gear plays up on the night. Think of a workaround in case something packs up. Play through

the PA? Use someone else's free amp channel? Take a
spare along?

Of course, having your kit serviced every so often
makes a lot of sense too, especially if you're using
vintage stuff. Find a local technician and get them to
look at your amp, keyboard or effect. Get them to blow
the dust out of vital bits, check for dry or intermittent
solder joints and replace any components that have
reached the end of their reliability.

For instance, one vintage item that's popular and
starting to get expensive these days is the Watkins
Copicat echo unit. When these are working they're a
great-sounding, flexible old tape echo. But even when
they were new they weren't exactly renowned for their
reliability and less so nowadays, when their components
have drifted out of whack and they've been carted
around in the back of vans for decades. One technician
who repairs them was brutally honest: "Whatever you
spend on a Copicat," he said, "be prepared to spend the
same again to make it roadworthy."

Much the same goes for other older gear – get it
checked and sorted before it suffers from an attack
of senile incontinence on stage and leaves you with
a box of crackling, useless electrics instead of a vital
part of your sound. If something's already starting to
act a little bit oddly in rehearsals, for goodness' sake
get it fixed before you step out in front of an audience.
Nothing kills the atmosphere like some nitwit noisily
fiddling with dodgy connections for ten minutes right
in the middle of a set.

Talking of reliability, decent cases are invaluable.
Whether it's fragile electronics, delicate instruments

or dentable drums, get your stuff in a good-quality case. Doubly so if you've got a van; a load of heavy, sloppily stacked gear crashing around in the back can reduce an unprotected instrument to splinters by the time you've exited the first roundabout. If you're utterly sure that your instrument will never leave your side or be treated roughly, a gigbag is fine; otherwise get it cased. The same goes for amp covers. Amps are fairly sturdy things, but the vinyl covers that come as standard are protection for scratches but not much else. You can pick up reinforced heavy-duty slip-on covers with boards to shield vulnerable bits for not much money. Certainly less than the cost of replacing a speaker or a set of valves.

Flight cases look properly professional, but are heavy and bulky – for most of us they're over-specified. Unless you're actually flying, of course, when the baggage handlers will do their utmost to make your gear into a heap of unrecognisable wreckage. When you peer out of a plane window and see your valuable vintage instrument being bounced across the tarmac, you'll be glad you spent a lot of money on a good flight case. Or you won't, in which case I hope your insurance is up to date.

So get your set-up down to a manageable minimum, get it reliable and keep it that way. Then you can concentrate on playing, which for most of us is actually the fun bit. Transport and logistics? Electrical troubleshooting? Emergency maintenance and repair? No thanks, I'd rather be out playing some music.

CHAPTER 10

INFORMATION INSPIRATION

Here comes the chewy bit. Throughout this book I've deliberately swerved away from throwing in links, footnotes and other addenda, for two reasons.

One is that it messes up the flow. I hate it when you get halfway through a sentence[1] and get dragged off to a different bit of the page* then have to find your place again.†

A second reason to give the dense facty bits their own chapter is that these change all the time. Many of them, being web links, will expire, shift, change address and generally wibble about. Books go out of print, magazines shut down or change ownership or direction. As for musical gear, it gets replaced or updated almost on a minute-by-minute basis. The DRG-7013 of last month will now be the DRG-7025e, which has four extra DPS sockets, two extra megaslabs of trunge-based swingless faddle memory and an improved TrugLok™ interface.

Keeping up to date with all that lot is a nightmare.

Then there's the fact that book publishing is necessarily a fairly slow operation; writing, editing,

1. Annoying isn't it?

* See above. Or below. Whatever.

† I bet you can't remember where you were now. I certainly can't.

checking, designing and publishing one of these things takes a good long while, and it's difficult to keep up to date during the time you're writing a book, let alone after it's been out on the shelves for a year or more.

So hopefully splitting this section off from the main body of the text will be easier to keep current in future editions; rather than trawling through the entire book we can just slot in a new, improved back section.

So here are a heap of places to go and things to explore. Almost everything you'll ever need to know is out there somewhere, either from a reputable mainstream source or, increasingly often, via some amazingly clued-up bod on an enthusiasts' forum.

And, of course, Google is your friend. Almost any question you can imagine has already been asked, and quite possibly answered, by somebody somewhere. A quick search will find even the most abstruse bit of information tucked down the back of the internet somewhere. So go forth and fill your brain.

BOOKS

It's difficult to pick out one particular book by a musical hero; there are a million autobiographies and biographies of stars, varying from squeaky-clean reputation-laundering jobs (mostly very dull) to warts-and-all tales of excess and bad behaviour (mostly very entertaining). You know what sort of musicians you admire and want to read about, so you'll already have your own ideas.

However, a few of the better stories of rock silliness include *No One Here Gets Out Alive* by Jerry Hopkins and Danny Sugarman, about The Doors' Jim Morrison,

Stephen Davis' Led Zeppelin book *Hammer of the Gods* and *The Dirt*, which dishes exactly that about big-haired hellraisers Mötley Crüe. Keith Richards' *Life* isn't bad either.

Also look out for British writer Barney Hoskyns, whose books on Californian '70s rock are surprisingly fascinating, even if you find James Taylor, Linda Ronstadt and so on a bit tedious. Charles Shaar Murray, John Harris and Richard Williams are other Brit authors well worth seeking out too.

If you're a guitar collector or enthusiast you should really own one of Tony Bacon's instrument bibles. Covering all the facts in magisterial depth and with very fine photography, they'll tell you more than you'll ever need to know about the history and development of a given brand or instrument. *The Ultimate Guitar Book* is a good place to start.

On a more practical note, it's time to slip in a shameless but well-deserved plug for our sister publications, the *Haynes Manuals*. Most instruments are covered in enormous detail, and there are more coming out all the time. If I told you which, they'd have to kill me, so keep an eye on the website to find out if your particular choice is already covered or scheduled to be shortly.

www.haynes.co.uk

MAGAZINES

Look on the shelves at your local newsagent, WH Smith or big supermarket and you'll find a fair few musicians' magazines. Of course many of them come in paperless formats too, offering websites and iPad apps with video and music too. Still, if you want something convenient to read on a plane, in the garden or on the loo it's difficult to beat a magazine. And if you want to get recent gear reviews, well-structured interviews and in-depth feature pieces all in one package, they're still somehow more satisfying than any amount of web surfing.

Guitarists are well catered for; there's plenty aimed at them.

Guitarist is the biggest, glossiest and probably most grown-up. Can slip into bland smugness, but it's not bad.
www.musicradar.com/guitarist

Guitar & Bass isn't bad either; sometimes has good coverage of musical instrument history too.
www.guitarmagazine.co.uk

Total Guitar is mostly aimed at young metalheads, and is full of bands with ridiculous clothing and pointy guitars that you won't have heard of. Occasionally has a decent song transcription, though.
www.musicradar.com/totalguitar

American magazine *Guitar Player* can be fiercely dull, though when it gets its teeth into a subject it does go into great depth.

Other American imports you may sometimes run across include *Guitar World* (a bit flimsy, though sometimes gets good interviews), *Premier Guitar* (similar, more hardware reviews), *Guitar Aficionado* (frankly weird, aimed at mega-rich collectors) and *Vintage Guitar,* which will satisfy your inner guitar geek with marvellously over-detailed features on guitars you'd probably never heard of, let alone played.

www.guitarplayer.com
www.guitarworld.com
www.premierguitar.com
www.guitaraficionado.com
www.vintageguitar.com

We really must slip in a mention of *Fretboard Journal* here. This subscription-only glossy is superbly produced and although it has a bit of a thing for acoustic American acts, it's a lovely object in its own right and does properly in-depth, well-photographed pieces on some legendary players and instruments.

www.fretboardjournal.com

Acoustic magazine does pretty much what it says on the tin, and isn't bad at all.

www.acousticmagazine.com

There's a US counterpart called *Acoustic Guitar* too, which is a bit earnest but quite in-depth.

www.acousticguitar.com

Bass players get a couple of magazines of their own, even if most of the guitar mags include a section too.

Bass Guitar is the UK's solitary bass-only offering, and is as focused as you'd imagine.
www.bassguitarmagazine.com

Bass Player is the well-respected American one, though like many US mags it can be a little dull at times.
www.bassplayer.com

Keyboard players, too, have their own publications; again, there are a few UK ones which have US counterparts.

Keyboard Player has been going for ages but at the time of writing was looking a bit shaky, and has gone online-only.
www.keyboardplayer.com

Keyboard magazine is the American one, and its website hosts a pretty decent forum.
www.keyboardmag.com

It's much the same story for drummers; a couple of publications serve that market.

Rhythm magazine is the UK best-seller, and is a good solid product.
www.musicradar.com/rhythm

Drummer is also pretty decent, and a little more lively.
   www.drummermagazine.co.uk

Modern Drummer is the long-running and widely respected American equivalent.
   www.moderndrummer.com

Then there's *Drum!* which, as you can tell from the exclamation mark, is a bit more excitable and younger. Also USA-based.
   www.drummagazine.com

If you're interested in recording, it's worth checking out these:

Recording magazine is aimed at the recording musician, so does good down-to-earth advice and reviews.
   www.recordingmag.com

Sound on Sound is a long-running and pretty in-depth publication, which is particularly good on synths and software.
   www.soundonsound.com

And it's definitely worth checking out a copy of *Tape Op* too. This American magazine is aimed at recording pros, but runs fantastically irreverent and entertaining features on what it's really like at the dirty end of the studio business. Has a very lively online forum as well, with many big names dropping by.

www.tapeop.com

Of course, this isn't everything by any means; from *Ukelele* magazine (www.ukuleleunlimited. com) to amusingly named organists' bible *The Organ* (www.theorganmag.com), there are a load of niche publications that can be subscribed to or hunted down in specialist shops. Thanks to the spiralling costs of print and paper and the slump in advertising sales, quite a few have gone online-only, but still keep up a solid presence aided by their readers, who have become forum members.

You may notice that several of the UK magazines' web addresses start with 'musicradar'. This (www. musicradar.com) is the combined online hub of Future Publishing's mags, and is a creditable stab at an all-you-can-eat musicians' website. There's plenty there for everybody and though the sheer breadth of material can occasionally make it a bit daunting to navigate, it's worth spending some time rummaging around in there. Which brings us to...

THE INTERNET

There's very little point listing every possible website here; that's what Google is for. Also, if we did that then this book would be the size of a double garage and use 14½ tons of paper. But here are a few favourites, either because they're useful or interesting.

INFORMATION INSPIRATION

Gumtree (www.gumtree.com) seems like a good option at the moment if you're looking for musicians or a band. It's free to list too, so you could try just putting an ad in on spec and seeing who turns up.

There are quite a few other musicians' noticeboards, some of which demand registration and/or money before posting your details or letting you browse listings. Unsurprisingly, these are less well populated than the free options, so think carefully before getting your wallet out. Here are a few of the more popular ones:

www.joinmyband.co.uk
www.bandmix.co.uk
www.partysounds.co.uk
www.formingbands.co.uk
www.musolist.com

If you're thinking of buying some gear and want to trawl through the big boys' websites, here are a few reasonable options. German megasite Thomann carry a huge range and can be cheap, but watch out for their delivery costs and minimum order values. The others are solid UK options, but there are plenty of others which a quick search will unearth. It's still worth trying your local shop first, however – they may offer to match online prices.

Thomann – www.thomann.de
GAK (Guitar, Amp, Keyboard – though they also do drums) – www.gak.co.uk
Dolphin Music – www.dolphinmusic.co.uk
Gear4music – www.gear4music.com

Building an online presence? Here are a few starting points. I'm sure you won't need help finding the well-known services like Facebook, Twitter or YouTube, but there are a few more music-specific ones that you might find useful.

MySpace, by web standards an ancient monument, has recently been given a spring-clean and is pretty good for musicians these days.
uk.myspace.com

Then there's Soundcloud, which is a good place to dump tracks, either for online collaboration, passing around between band members or playing to other people.
www.soundcloud.com

And Dropbox is worth investigating for its free online storage; it's another good way of sharing demos, rehearsal recordings and other sizeable files.
www.dropbox.com

If you're having ear trouble, you're not alone. Here's an organisation with strong music links who might be able to help: the British Tinnitus Association.
www.tinnitus.org.uk
And, finally, these people are nothing to do with us, but they're trying to put together an online community for older musicians. As yet it's a little sparsely populated, but take a look – and if you join up, maybe it'll become a massive success.
www.rock-til-you-drop.com